Doctrine Matters

Ten Theological Trademarks from a Lifetime of Preaching

from John Piper

Published by Desiring God
Post Office Box 2901
Minneapolis, MN 55402
www.desiringGod.org

Cover design and typesetting
Taylor Design Works

All emphases in Scripture quotations have been added by the author or editor.

TABLE OF CONTENTS

EDITOR'S PREFACE

Systematic theology is glorious.

We know who God is. He has told us. In fact, he has spoken so clearly through the Bible that we can produce volumes of faithful literature about who he is and who he's not, how he acts and how he doesn't, and what it all means for life. We have these books, some better than others, that have been given to the church for thousands of years. We should read them and learn. We should thank God for them.

And then there is preaching.

There is the week in, week out exposition of God's word to a particular people in a particular time with a particular vision. This is where the theology is proclaimed and celebrated. It's where the truth of God is held out for real people, for Gary and Lisa, for Ms. Verna, for Joel, for Mike and Emily, for you and me.

The preaching, you could say, is where the rubber begins to meet the road on what a church believes. It is the living statement of faith. Most of us get to see only seasons of this unfold in the course of a pastor's ministry. A few people get to experience the whole thing from the pews. And then, in the case of John Piper, we have online every sermon he's ever preached, for free, including a ten-part series where he devotes a single message to the main theological emphases of his 32-year preaching tenure.

Piper himself, reflecting on three decades of pastoral ministry, has extracted the most essential emphases he wants to reiterate and bequeath to the flock and leadership at Bethlehem Baptist Church in the Twin Cities. Piper titled this series "Thirty-Year Theological Trademarks." These ten sermons, preached at the end of 2012, are in large measure Piper's theological legacy manifest in and cherished by a local church. But though the legacy is local, its impact reaches much broader. The theology here is for God's people everywhere, and that's why this book exists.

How to Use This Book

The original sermon series has been reorganized into a more systematic outline, including edits that help the individual sermons read more like chapters. We've also removed little things particular to Bethlehem and added headers with the hopes of giving this resource dual functionality.

You can read each sermon through as stand-alone chapters. Or, because the subject headers within each chapter are found in the Table of Contents, you can reference specific portions that have in-the-moment interest for you. Whether to answer pressing questions or to provide devotional fodder, the hope is that this Table of Contents will serve you.

You will also notice that each chapter includes a section of additional excerpts from Piper on the particular topic. David Mathis, Tony Reinke, and I teamed up for a deep dive into Piper's 1,200-plus sermons since 1980 to select some of the best excerpts that re-highlight each doctrinal emphasis. The letters A to J signal these chapter appendices, which are also found in the Table of Contents for your reference ease.

Doctrine Matters, Really

Before you get into the meat of this book, there are two important things to keep in mind.

First, this book is about matters of doctrine—"theological trademarks" as Piper calls them. But that doesn't mean they are new. "They're not distinctive to us." They're not niche or eccentric. "[These doctrines] all have wide foundations in the Bible and deep roots in the history of God's people," Piper explains.

> *When we say "trademarks" we mean truths that are defining and shaping and precious. We don't mean views that we've come up with and that set us off from the rest of the church of Christ. We don't want to be set off. We want to be arm in arm with millions of faithful followers of God's word. Truth does divide. But it also unites. And it is the uniting power of truth that we delight in most. (from Chapter 5, Section 1)*

Second, the doctrines in this book matter. They really matter. Don't think that these sermons are the memoirs of a retired pastor. Don't think that these truths can be shelved away to collect dust. The vision of God in these pages doesn't take a pat on the head—it turns the world upside down.

These doctrines are, as Piper says, "wildly untamable, explosively uncontainable, and electrically future-creating." They make a difference.

So consider this an encouragement, and a caution. When you read these truths and immerse yourself in this biblical vision of our great God, you will want to act. You will want to build something. You will want to start things. You will be compelled to dream big and risk bigger for the glory of Jesus Christ. And we pray for nothing less.

Jonathan Parnell
desiringGod.org

1. GOD IS

> *Then Moses said to God, "If I come to the people of Israel and say to them, 'The God of your fathers has sent me to you,' and they ask me, 'What is his name?' what shall I say to them?"* [14] *God said to Moses, "I Am Who I Am." And he said, "Say this to the people of Israel, 'I Am has sent me to you.'"* [15] *God also said to Moses, "Say this to the people of Israel, 'The Lord, the God of your fathers, the God of Abraham, the God of Isaac, and the God of Jacob, has sent me to you.' This is my name forever, and thus I Am to be remembered throughout all generations.*
> —Exodus 3:13–15

My ultimate goal in the ten chapters of this book is to spread a passion for the supremacy of God in all things for the joy of all peoples through Jesus Christ. In other words, I aim to make so much of God the Father, and God the Son, through God the Spirit, that you—and thousands through you—will be moved to join me in glad adoration of our triune God.

Under that overarching aim, my goal is to awaken and strengthen a strong conviction in you that the last 30 years of ministry at Bethlehem Baptist Church have been preparation, not consummation. Or to put it another way, I hope to help you see and feel that my transition as the Pastor for Preaching at Bethlehem is less about landing and more about launching. It is less about the great things God has done, and more about the greater things God is going to do.

Therefore it has seemed good to me, with the encouragement of the pastoral staff of Bethlehem, to turn our attention to a battery of foundational realities—defining truths, thirty-year trademarks, biblical touchstones—that have profoundly shaped what Bethlehem Baptist Church is for these last three decades.

1.1 Future-Creating Realities

The summary of foundational truths in this book is like a launch rather than land. They lead us to pursue preparation rather than ponder consummation, to lay hold on the greater things to come rather than lingering over the great things of the past. The reason is that these foundational realities, expounded in each chapter, are wildly untamable, and explosively uncontainable, and electrically future-creating. They don't just sustain the present and explain the past. They are living and active and supernaturally supercharged to take this church where it has not yet dreamed, in ways we have not yet dreamed.

And I should make clear before I launch into the launch with these explosive truths, that I have little doubt in my mind—and the little doubt in my mind is not of God, but of a lack of God—that the next season of Bethlehem's life will be the greatest we've ever known. We all know that many ministries have flourished for decades and become significant, and then with a leadership change, things fall apart and impact wanes, and hope fades, and joy departs, and the ministry dwindles, and maybe even dies. My deep conviction is that God is not going to let that happen at Bethlehem. In fact, if I had to, I'd stake my life on that prediction.

And so we turn to this battery of foundational realities—these defining truths, these 30-year trademarks, these biblical touchstones—that have shaped what Bethlehem is for these last three decades, these wildly untamable, explosively uncontainable, and electrically future-creating realities.

1.2 God Absolutely Is

The first theological trademark is that *God is*. Or to say it the way our text says it, *God is who he is*. Or to say it more philosophically, *God absolutely is*. This is the most basic fact and the most ultimate fact. Period. Of the billions of facts that there are, this one is at the bottom and at the top. It is the foundation of all others and the consummation of all others. Nothing is more basic and nothing is more ultimate than the fact that *God is*.

Nothing is more foundational than that *God is*. Nothing is more foundational to your life or your marriage or your job or your health or your mind or your future than that *God is*. Nothing is more foundational to the world, or the solar system, or the Milky Way or the universe than that *God is*. And nothing is more foundational to the Bible and the self-revelation of God and the glory of the gospel of Jesus than that *God is*.

1.3 Understanding Exodus 3

The reality that *God absolutely is* stands as the point of Exodus 3:13–15. Let me set the stage for you. For several centuries the people of Israel—God's chosen people—have lived as aliens in Egypt. And for a long time they have been treated as slaves. Now the time of God's deliverance is drawing near. A Jewish child is born, named Moses. He is providentially rescued from the edict of death by Pharaoh's daughter and raised in the court. As an adult he defends one of his kinsman by killing an Egyptian, and flees to the land of Midian. And there God appears to him in a burning bush, as we read in Exodus 3:6–10:

> *He said, "I Am the God of your father, the God of Abraham, the God of Isaac, and the God of Jacob." And Moses hid his face, for he was afraid to look at God.* [7] *Then the Lord said, "I have surely seen the affliction of my people who are in Egypt and have heard their cry because of their taskmasters. I know their sufferings,* [8] *and I have come down to deliver them out of the hand of the Egyptians and to bring them up out of that land to a good and broad land, a land flowing with milk and honey, to the place of the Canaanites, the Hittites, the Amorites, the Perizzites, the Hivites, and the Jebusites.* [9] *And now, behold, the cry of the people of Israel has come to me,*

> *and I have also seen the oppression with which the Egyptians oppress them.* [10] *Come, I will send you to Pharaoh that you may bring my people, the children of Israel, out of Egypt."*

So Moses is God's chosen leader to bring his people out of slavery and into the promised land. But he shrinks back. As well he might—or Jason might, or you might. Verse 11: "But Moses said to God, 'Who am I that I should go to Pharaoh and bring the children of Israel out of Egypt?'" And God said (verse 12), "But I will be with you, and this shall be the sign for you, that I have sent you: when you have brought the people out of Egypt, you shall serve God on this mountain."

And then Moses brings us to one of the most important things God ever said. This is our text, Exodus 3:13–15:

> *Then Moses said to God, "If I come to the people of Israel and say to them, 'The God of your fathers has sent me to you,' and they ask me, 'What is his name?' What shall I say to them?"* [14] *God said to Moses, "I Am Who I Am." And he said, "Say this to the people of Israel, 'I Am has sent me to you.'"* [15] *God also said to Moses, "Say this to the people of Israel, 'The Lord [Hebrew: "Yahweh"], the God of your fathers, the God of Abraham, the God of Isaac, and the God of Jacob, has sent me to you.' This is my name forever [Yahweh], and thus I Am to be remembered throughout all generations."*

1.4 Three Things God Says About Himself

You ask me my name, God says, I will tell you three things. First (verse 14) "God said to Moses, 'I Am Who I Am.'" He did not say that was his name. He said, in effect: Before you worry about my name, where I line up among the many God's of Egypt or Babylon or Philistia, and before you wonder about conjuring me with my name, and even before you wonder if I Am the God of Abraham, be stunned by this: "I Am Who I Am." I absolutely am. Before you get my name, get my being. That I Am Who I Am—that I absolutely Am—is first, foundational, and of infinite importance.

Second (verse 14b) "And he said, 'Say this to the people of Israel, "I Am has sent me to you."'" Here he has not yet given Moses his name. He is building a bridge between his being and his name. Here he simply puts the statement of his being in the place of his name. Say, "I Am has sent me to you." The one who is—who absolutely is—sent me to you.

Third (verse 15) "God also said to Moses, 'Say this to the people of Israel, "The Lord [Hebrew: "Yahweh"], the God of your fathers, the God of Abraham, the God of Isaac, and the God of Jacob, has sent me to you." This is my name forever [Yahweh]. Finally he gives us his name. It's almost always translated Lord (all caps) in the English Bible. But the Hebrew would be pronounced something like "Yahweh," and is built on the word for "I Am." So every time we hear the word Yahweh (or the short form Yah, which you hear every time you sing "hallelu-jah", "praise Yahweh"), or every time you see Lord in the English Bible you should think: this is a proper name (like Peter or James or John) built out of the word for "I Am" and reminding us each time that God absolutely is.

1.5 The Truth Makes an Irrepressible People

God absolutely is. This is amazing. God gave himself a name (used over 4,000 times in the Old Testament) that presses us, when we hear it to think, He is. He absolutely is. He is absolute.

This is the first of the battery of foundational realities—defining truths, thirty-year trademarks, biblical touchstones—that have marked Bethlehem Baptist Church for three decades. We are blown away by the sheer fact that God is. That "he is who he is." That he absolutely is. This is the first of the wildly untamable, explosively uncontainable, electrically future-creating realities that we embrace.

A people who are stunned that God is will be an irrepressible people. Our triune God loves to show up in gracious power where people are blown away by the fact that he is.

1.6 Ten Things It Means for God to Be Who He Is

What does it mean for God to be who he is? Here are ten points:

1. God's absolute being means he never had a beginning. This staggers the mind. Every child asks, "Who made God?" And every wise parent says, "Nobody made God. God simply is. And always was. No beginning."

2. God's absolute being means God will never end. If he did not come into being, he cannot go out of being

because he is being. He is what is. There is no place to go outside of being. There is only he. Before he creates, that's all that is: God.

3. God's absolute being means God is absolute reality. There is no reality before him. There is no reality outside of him unless he wills it and makes it. He is not one of many realities before he creates. He is simply there as absolute reality. He is all that was eternally. No space, no universe, no emptiness. Only God. Absolutely there. Absolutely all.

4. God's absolute being means that God is utterly independent. He depends on nothing to bring him into being or support him or counsel him or make him what he is. That is what the words "absolute being" mean.

5. God's absolute being means rather that everything that is not God depends totally on God. All that is not God is secondary, and dependent. The entire universe is utterly secondary. Not primary. It came into being by God and stays in being moment by moment on God's decision to keep it in being.

6. God's absolute being means all the universe is by comparison to God as nothing. Contingent, dependent reality is to absolute, independent reality as a shadow to substance. As an echo to a thunderclap. As a bubble to the ocean. All that we see, all that we are amazed by in the world and in the galaxies, is, compared to God, as nothing. "All the nations are as nothing before him, they are accounted by him as less than nothing and emptiness" (Isaiah 40:17).

7. God's absolute being means that God is constant. He is the same yesterday, today, and forever. He cannot be improved. He is not becoming anything. He is who he is. There is no development in God. No progress. Absolute perfection cannot be improved.

8. God's absolute being means that he is the absolute standard of truth and goodness and beauty. There is no law-book to which he looks to know what is right. No almanac to establish facts. No guild to determine what is excellent or beautiful. He himself is the standard of what is right, what is true, what is beautiful.

9. God's absolute being means God does whatever he pleases and it is always right and always beautiful and always in accord with truth. There are no constraints on him from outside him that could hinder him in doing anything he pleases. All reality that is outside of him he created and designed and governs as the absolute reality. So he is utterly free from any constraints that don't originate from the counsel of his own will.

10. God's absolute being means that he is the most important and most valuable reality and the most important and most valuable person in the universe. He is more worthy of interest and attention and admiration and enjoyment than all other realities, including the entire universe.

1.7 The Cosmic Outrage

God absolutely is! We believe and cherish this. God is. It is a wildly untamable, explosively uncontainable, electrically future-creating reality—that God is.

Therefore, it is a cosmic outrage billions of times over that God is ignored, treated as negligible, questioned, criticized, treated as virtually nothing, and given less thought than the carpet in people's houses.

Being the most significant reality there is, nothing is rightly known apart from its relationship to him. He is the source and goal and definer of all beings and all things.

We will, therefore, be a God-besotted people. To know him, to admire him, to make him known as glorious is our driving passion. He is simply, overwhelmingly dominant in our consciousness. All must be related to him if we exist to spread a passion for the supremacy of God!

1.8 Never Make God Peripheral

God helping us, we will not blaspheme him. We will not blaspheme the God who absolutely is by taking him for granted, or making him peripheral, or calling him the assumed foundation of all the things while it's the "things" we are really excited about. We dread ever falling under the criticism of Albert Einstein that Charles Misner wrote about twenty years ago:

> *I do see the design of the universe as essentially a religious question. That is, one should have some kind of respect and awe for the whole business.... It's very magnificent and shouldn't be taken for granted. In fact, I believe that is why Einstein had so little use for organized religion, although he strikes me as a basically very religious man. He must have looked at what the preachers said about God and felt that they*

were blaspheming. He had seen much more majesty than they had ever imagined, and they were just not talking about the real thing. (Quoted in First Things, *Dec. 1991, No. 18, 63)*

When I read that, I said, "O God, never, never let that happen at Bethlehem!" There are thousands of people in this city and billions in the world who are starving to know the true and living God who absolutely is. And we have the good news that this God has sent his Son into the world to die for God-belittling sinners like us so that whoever believes in Jesus Christ may know this God with joy forever. So we know our calling. We exist to spread a passion for God who absolutely is.

This is where we've been. This is where we are going. Untamable, uncontainable, this is an electrically future-creating reality. "I Am Who I Am." God absolutely is.

A. MORE ABOUT GOD

Seven Glorious Truths About God in Isaiah 6

In the year that King Uzziah died I saw the Lord sitting upon a throne, high and lifted up; and the train of his robe filled the temple. Above him stood the seraphim. Each had six wings: with two he covered his face, and with two he covered his feet, and with two he flew. And one called to another and said: "Holy, holy, holy is the Lord of hosts; the whole earth is full of his glory!" And the foundations of the thresholds shook at the voice of him who called, and the house was filled with smoke. —Isaiah 6:1–4

Here are seven glimpses of God I see in these four verses:

Glimpse #1: God Is Alive

First, he is *alive*. In the year that king Uzziah died. Uzziah is dead, but God lives on. "From everlasting to everlasting, thou art God" (Psalm 90:2). God was the living God when this universe banged into existence. He was the living God when Socrates drank his poison. He was the living God when William Bradford governed Plymouth Colony. He was the living God in 1966 when Thomas Altizer proclaimed him dead and *Time* magazine put it on the front cover. And he will be the living God ten trillion ages from now when all the puny potshots against his reality will have sunk into oblivion like BB's at the bottom of the Pacific Ocean.

"In the year that king Uzziah died I saw the Lord." There is not a single head of state in all the world who will be there in fifty years. The turnover in world leadership is 100%. But not God. He never had a beginning and therefore depends on nothing for his existence. He always has been and always will be alive.

Glimpse #2: God Is Authoritative

Second, he is *authoritative*. "I saw the Lord sitting upon a *throne*." No vision of heaven has ever caught a glimpse of God plowing a field or cutting his grass or shining shoes or filling out reports or loading a truck. Heaven is not coming apart at the seams by inattention. God is never at wits' end with his heavenly realm. He sits. And he sits on a *throne*. All is at peace and he has control.

The throne is his right to rule the world. We do not give God authority over our lives. He has it whether we like it or not. What utter folly it is to act as though we had any rights at all to call God into question! We need to hear, now and then, blunt words like those of Virginia Stem Owens who said in the *Reformed Journal*:

> *Let us get this one thing straight. God can do anything he damn well pleases, including damn well. And if it pleases him to damn, then it is done, ipso facto, well. God's activity is what it is. There isn't anything else. Without it there would be no being, including human beings presuming to judge the Creator of everything that is.*

Few things are more humbling, few things give us that sense of raw majesty, as the truth that God is utterly *authoritative* does. He is the Supreme Court, the Legislature, and the Chief Executive. After him, no appeal.

Glimpse #3: God Is Omnipotent

Third, God is *omnipotent*. The throne of his authority is not one among many. It is high and lifted up. "I saw the Lord sitting upon a throne high and lifted up." That God's throne is higher than every other throne signifies God's superior power to exercise his authority. No opposing authority can nullify the decrees of God. What he purposes, he accomplishes. "My counsel shall stand, and I will accomplish all my purpose" (Isaiah 46:10). "He does according to his will in the host of heaven and among the inhabitants of the earth; and none can stay his hand" (Daniel 4:35). And this sovereign authority of the living God is a refuge full of joy and power for those who keep his covenant.

Glimpse #4: God Is Resplendent

Fourth, God is *resplendent.* "I saw the Lord sitting upon a throne high and lifted up, *and his train filled the temple.*" You have seen pictures of brides whose dresses are gathered around them covering the steps and the platform. What would the meaning be if the train filled the aisles and covered the seats and the choir loft, woven all of one piece? That God's robe fills the entire heavenly temple means that he is a God of incomparable splendor. The fullness of God's splendor shows itself in a thousand ways.

I used to read *Ranger Rick.* I recall an article on species of fish who live deep in the dark sea and have their own built-in lights—some have lamps hanging from their chins, some have luminescent noses, some have beacons under their eyes. There are a thousand kinds of self-lighted fish who live deep in the ocean where none of us can see and marvel. They are spectacularly weird and beautiful. Why are they there? Why not just a dozen or so efficient streamlined models? Because God is lavish in splendor. His creative fullness spills over in excessive beauty. And if that's the way the world is, how much more resplendent must be the Lord who thought it up and made it!

Glimpse #5: God Is Revered

Fifth, God is *revered*. "Above him stood the seraphim; each had six wings: with two he covered his face, and with two he covered his feet, and with two he flew." No one knows what these strange six-winged creatures with feet and eyes and intelligence are. They never appear again in the Bible—at least not under the name seraphim. Given the grandeur of the scene and the power of the angelic hosts, we had best not picture chubby winged babies fluttering about the Lord's ears. According to verse 4, when one of them speaks, the foundations of the temple shake. We would do better to think of the Blue Angels—those four jets that fly in formation—diving in formation before the presidential entourage and cracking the sound barrier just before his face. There are no puny or silly creatures in heaven. Only magnificent ones.

And the point is: not even they can look upon the Lord nor do they feel worthy even to leave their feet exposed in his presence. Great and good as they are, untainted by human sin, they revere their Maker in great humility. An angel terrifies a man with his brilliance and power. But angels themselves hide in holy fear and reverence from the splendor of God. He is continually revered.

Glimpse #6: God Is Holy

Sixth, God is *holy*. "And one called to another, 'Holy, holy, holy is the Lord of hosts!'" Language is pushing its limits of usefulness here. The effort to define the holiness of God ultimately winds up by saying: God is holy means God is God.

Let me illustrate. The root meaning of holy is probably

to cut or separate. A *holy thing* is cut off from and separated from common (we would say secular) use. Earthly things and persons are holy as they are distinct from the world and devoted to God. So the Bible speaks of holy ground (Exodus 3:5), holy assemblies (Exodus 12:16), holy sabbaths (Exodus 16:23), a holy nation (Exodus 19:6), holy garments (Exodus 28:2), a holy city (Nehemiah 11:1), holy promises (Psalm 105:42), holy men (2 Peter 1:21) and women (1 Peter 3:5), holy scriptures (2 Timothy 3:15), holy hands (1 Timothy 2:8), a holy kiss (Romans 16:16), and a holy faith (Jude 20). Almost anything can become holy if it is separated from the common and devoted to God.

But notice what happens when this definition is applied to God himself. From what can you separate God to make him holy? The very god-ness of God means that he is separate from all that is not God. There is an infinite qualitative difference between Creator and creature. God is one of a kind. Sui generis. In a class by himself. In that sense he is utterly holy. But then you have said no more than that he is God.

Or if the holiness of a man derives from being separated from the world and devoted to God, to whom is God devoted so as to derive his holiness? To no one but himself. It is blasphemy to say that there is a higher reality than God to which he must conform in order to be holy. God is the absolute reality beyond which is only more of God. When asked for his name in Exodus 3:14, he said, "I am who I am." His being and his character are utterly undetermined by anything outside himself. He is not holy because he keeps the rules. He wrote the rules! God is not holy because he keeps the law. The law is holy because it reveals God. God is absolute. Everything else is derivative.

What then is his holiness? It is his infinite worth. His holiness is his utterly unique divine essence, which in his uniqueness has infinite value. It determines all that he is and does and is determined by no one. His holiness is what he is as God, which no one else is or ever will be. Call it his majesty, his divinity, his greatness, his value as the pearl of great price.

In the end language runs out. In the word "holy" we have sailed to the world's end in the utter silence of reverence and wonder and awe. There may yet be more to know of God, but that will be beyond words. "The Lord is in his holy temple; let all the earth keep silence before him" (Habakkuk 2:20).

Glimpse #7: God Is Glorious

But before the silence and the shaking of the foundations and the all-concealing smoke, we learn a seventh and final thing about God. God is glorious. "Holy, holy, holy is the Lord of hosts, the whole earth is full of his glory."

The glory of God is the manifestation of his holiness. God's holiness is the incomparable perfection of his divine nature; his glory is the display of that holiness. "God is glorious" means God's holiness has gone public. His glory is the open revelation of the secret of his holiness. In Leviticus 10:3 God says, "I will show myself *holy* among those who are near me, and before all the people I will be *glorified*." When God shows himself to be holy, what we see is glory. The holiness of God is his concealed glory. The glory of God is his revealed holiness.

Now, what does this have to do with the gospel of Jesus Christ incarnate as the God-Man and crucified and risen from the dead at the center of history?

The gospel of John makes the connections for us more clearly than anyone, in John 12. And I will put it in a very brief statement. In Isaiah 6, Isaiah presents God as high and holy and majestic and authoritative and sovereign and resplendent, and God says in verse 10 that this message will harden the people. They do not want such a God. But the chapter ends with a reference to a stump of faithfulness that remains, and Isaiah speaks of a "holy seed" (verse 13).

In Isaiah 53 that seed is described as the suffering servant who had "no form or majesty that we should look at him, and no beauty that we should desire him. He was despised and rejected by men" (Isaiah 53:2–3). Just the opposite of the picture of God in Isaiah 6.

But Isaiah 53:1 says they rejected that message as well: "Who has believed what he has heard from us?" (Isaiah 53:1).

These are the very two texts that John quotes in reference to the rejection of Jesus in John 12:38 and 40. Why? John tells us in Isaiah 12:41, "Isaiah said these things because he saw his glory and spoke of him" (John 12:41).

In other words, Jesus was the fulfillment of both the majesty of Isaiah 6 and the misery of Isaiah 53. And that, John says, is why he was rejected. He came to his own and his own did not receive him. Why? Because Jesus was the glory of Isaiah 6 and the suffering servant of Isaiah 53. John says so in John 12:41, "Isaiah said these things because he saw his glory and spoke of him."

We beheld his glory, glory of the only Son from the

Father full of grace and truth and that glory was the unprecedented mingling of the majesty of Isaiah 6 and the misery of Isaiah 53.

And why was this incomparable Christ rejected? John gives the answer in John 12:43, "The people loved the glory that comes from man more than the glory that comes from God."

And because they loved human glory more than divine glory they rejected Jesus—the embodiment of the glory of God, both in his greatness as God and his lowliness as the suffering servant.

But all this was part of God's design. The Son of Man came not to be served but to serve and give his life a ransom for many. His rejection was the plan. Because his death for sinners was the plan.

Does he then abandon his people Israel because they rejected him? No. That too is part of the plan. "A partial hardening has come upon Israel, until the fullness of the Gentiles has come in. And in this way all Israel will be saved" (Romans 11:25–26).

Or as Romans 11:31 says, "So Israel too has been disobedient in order that by the mercy shown to you Gentiles they also may now receive mercy" (Romans 11:31). Nothing has been wasted. There were no detours on the way to this great salvation of all God's elect.

And when Paul stands back and looks at the whole plan, he worships:

> *Oh, the depth of the riches and wisdom and knowledge of God! How unsearchable are his judgments and how inscrutable his ways! "For who*

> *has known the mind of the Lord, or who has been his counselor? Or who has given a gift to him that he might be repaid?" For from him and through him and to him are all things. To him be glory forever. Amen."* —Romans 11:33–36

This is our God.

2. THE GLORY OF GOD

But now thus says the Lord, he who created you, O Jacob, he who formed you, O Israel: "Fear not, for I have redeemed you; I have called you by name, you are mine.
² When you pass through the waters, I will be with you; and through the rivers, they shall not overwhelm you; when you walk through fire you shall not be burned, and the flame shall not consume you.
³ For I am the Lord your God, the Holy One of Israel, your Savior. I give Egypt as your ransom, Cush and Seba in exchange for you.
⁴ Because you are precious in my eyes, and honored, and I love you, I give men in return for you, peoples in exchange for your life.
⁵ Fear not, for I am with you; I will bring your offspring from the east, and from the west I will gather you.
⁶ I will say to the north, Give up, and to the south, Do not withhold; bring my sons from afar and my daughters from the end of the earth,
⁷ everyone who is called by my name, whom I

created for my glory, whom I formed and made."
— Isaiah 43:1–7

After the question in Chapter 1, "Does God exist?"—to which God answers, "I Am" (Exodus 3:14)—the next question that has shaped us most deeply is: "Why did God create the world?"

The short answer that resounds through the whole Bible like rolling thunder is: *God created the world for his glory.* We'll talk in a moment what that means, but let's establish the fact first.

Notice the key verses in Isaiah 43:6b–7, "Bring my sons from afar and my daughters from the end of the earth, everyone who is called by my name, whom *I created for my glory*, whom I formed and made." Even if the most narrow meaning here is "I brought Israel into being for my glory" the use of the words "created," "formed," and "made" are pointing us back to the original act of creation. This is why Israel *ultimately* exists. Because this is why all things ultimately exist—for the glory of God.

2.1 The Bible Is Clear About the Glory of God

When the first chapter of the Bible says, "So God created man *in his own image*, in the *image of God* he created him; male and female he created them" (Genesis 1:27), what is the point? The point of an image is *to image*. Images are erected to display the original. Point to the original. Glorify the original. God made humans in his image so that the world would be filled with reflectors of God. Images of God. Six billion statues of God. So that nobody would miss the point of creation. Nobody (unless they were stone-blind) could miss the point of humanity, namely, God. Knowing, loving, showing God.

The angels cry in Isaiah 6:3, "Holy, holy, holy is the Lord of hosts; *the whole earth is full of his glory*!" It's full of millions of human image bearers. Glorious ruins. But not only humans. Also nature! Why such a breathtaking world for us to live in? Why such a vast universe. I read the other day (can't verify it!) that there are more stars in the universe than there are words and sounds that all humans of all time have ever spoken. Why?

The Bible is crystal clear about this: "The heavens declare the glory of God" (Psalm 19:1). If someone asks, "If earth is the only inhabited planet and man the only rational inhabitant among the stars, why such a large and empty universe?" The answer is: It's not about us. It's about God. And that's an understatement. God created us to know him and love him and show him. And then he gave us a hint of what he is like —the universe.

The universe is declaring the glory of God and the reason we exist is to see it and be stunned by it and glorify God because of it. So Paul says in Romans 1:20–21,

> *His invisible attributes, namely, his eternal power and divine nature, have been clearly perceived, ever since the creation of the world, in the things that have been made. So they are without excuse. For although they knew God, they did not glorify him as God.*

The great tragedy of the universe is that while human beings were made to glorify God, we have all fallen short of this purpose and "exchanged the glory of the immortal God for images resembling mortal man" (Romans

1:23)—especially the one in the mirror. This is the essence of what we call sin.

So, why did God create the universe? Resounding through the whole Bible—from eternity to eternity—like rolling thunder is: God created the world for his glory.

2.2 Isaiah's Testimony to the Glory of God

Isaiah states plainly in Isaiah 43:7 that God created the world for his glory. He goes on to press home the reality over and over to help us feel it and make it part of the fabric of our thinking:

› Isaiah 40:4–5, "Every valley shall be lifted up, and every mountain and hill be made low; ... And *the glory of the Lord shall be revealed*, and all flesh shall see it together, for the mouth of the Lord has spoken."

› Isaiah 42:8, "I am the Lord; that is my name; my glory I give to no other, nor my praise to carved idols."

› Isaiah 44:23, "Break forth into singing, O mountains, O forest, and every tree in it! For the Lord has redeemed Jacob, and will be glorified in Israel."

› Isaiah 48:9–11, "For my name's sake I defer my anger, for the sake of my praise I restrain it for you... I have tried you in the furnace of affliction. For my own sake, for my own sake, I do it, for how should my name be profaned? My glory I will not give to another."

› Isaiah 49:3, "And he said to me, 'You are my servant, Israel, in whom I will be glorified.'"

- Isaiah 60:2, "For behold, darkness shall cover the earth, and thick darkness the peoples; but the Lord will arise upon you, and his glory will be seen upon you."
- Isaiah 61:1–3, "The Spirit of the Lord God is upon me, because the Lord has anointed me to bring good news to the poor; ... to give them... the garment of praise instead of a faint spirit; that they may be called oaks of righteousness, the planting of the Lord, that he may be glorified."

2.3 How "Glorify" Is Different from "Beautify"

God created the world "that he may be glorified." Which does not mean: "that he may be *made* glorious." Don't take the word "glorify" and treat it like the word "beautify." To beautify means to take a plain room and make it beautiful. We don't take a plain God and make him beautiful. That is not what glorifying God means.

When God created the world he did not create out of any need or any weakness or any deficiency. He created out of fullness and strength and complete sufficiency. As Jonathan Edwards said, "Tis no argument of the emptiness or deficiency of a fountain that it is inclined to overflow" (Yale: *Works*, Vol. 8, 448). So we don't glorify God by improving his glory, but by seeing and savoring and showing his glory (which is the same as knowing, loving, showing).

Or switch to the word "magnify" (so Philippians 1:20, "that Christ be magnified," *megalunthesetai*). We magnify his glory like a telescope not a microscope. Microscopes make small things look bigger than they are. Telescopes make unimaginably big things look more like what they really are. Our lives are to be telescopes for the glory of God. We were created to see his glory, be thrilled by his glory, and live so as to help others see him and savor him for what he really is. To know, to love, to show his glory.

That is why the universe exists. If this takes hold of you the way it should, it will affect the way you think and feel about everything. Now you know why everything exists. You don't know everything. There are billions of things you don't know. But you are never at a loss to know something important about everything. Because you know that everything exists for the glory of God. You know something about everything. And this is one of the most important things you can know about anything. And so to know this one thing—that all things exist for the glory of God—is to know something supremely important about everything. Namely, for what purpose it ultimately exists. That is amazing.

2.4 Why Did God Make *This* Particular World?

To just say God created the world for his glory is too general. We can't leave it here. It's too disconnected from the specific persons of the Trinity and from the flow of history the way God is guiding it. The question is not just, "Why did God create the world?" but why this world?—why these thousands of years of human history with a glorious beginning, and a horrible fall into sin, and a history of Israel, and the coming of the Son of God into the world, a substitutionary death, a triumphant resurrection, the founding of the church and the history of global missions to where we are today? Why this world? This history?

And the short answer to that question is, *for the glory of God's grace displayed supremely in the death of Jesus.* Or to say it more fully: This world—this history as it is unfolding—was created and is guided and sustained by God so that the grace of God, supremely displayed in the death and resurrection of Jesus for sinners would be glorified throughout all eternity in the Christ-exalting joys of the redeemed. Or let's just keep it short: this world exists for the glory of God's grace revealed in the saving work of Jesus. Which means that Bethlehem is not just a God-centered church, but a Christ-exalting church and a gospel-driven church. For us there is an unbreakable connection between the glory of God, the glory of grace, the glory of Christ, the glory of the cross.

2.5 Five Points on God's Glory and Christ's Cross

Let me show you, from the Bible, how God's glory is connected to the cross of Christ. We can do it in five steps.

1. The apex—the high point—of God's display of his own glory is the *display of his grace.*

"God predestined us for adoption as sons through Jesus Christ, according to the purpose of his will, to the praise of the glory of his grace" (Ephesians 1:5–6). In other words, the glory of God's *grace*—what Paul calls "the riches of his grace in kindness toward us in Christ Jesus" (Ephesians 2:7)—is the highpoint and endpoint in the revelation of

God's glory. And the aim of predestination is that we live to the praise of the glory of this grace forever.

This is the endpoint of his glory, and everything else, even God's wrath serves this. So Paul says in Romans 9:22–23, "Desiring to show his wrath and to make known his power, God has endured with much patience vessels of wrath... *in order to make known the riches of his glory for vessels of mercy*." Wrath is penultimate. The glory of grace on the vessels of mercy is ultimate.

2. God planned this—the praise of the glory of his grace—*before creation.*

"God chose us in him *before the foundation of the world...* to the praise of the glory of his grace" (Ephesians 1:4, 6). Grace was not an afterthought in response to the fall of man. It was the plan, because grace is the summit of the mountain of his glory. And he created the world for his glory. He planned the world for the glory of his grace.

3. God's plan was that the praise of the glory of his grace would come about *through the Son of God, Jesus Christ.*

"He predestined us for adoption as sons *through Jesus Christ...* to the praise of the glory of his grace" (Ephesians 1:5–6). This predestination to the praise of the glory of God's grace happened "through Jesus Christ." In the eternal fellowship of the Trinity, the Father and the Son planned that God's grace would be supremely revealed through the saving work of the Son.

Again, Paul says in 2 Timothy 1:9, "God called us to a holy calling, not because of our works but because of his own purpose and *grace*, which he gave us *in Christ Jesus* before the ages began." So, before the ages of time began, the plan was for the revelation of the glory of the grace of God specifically through Christ Jesus.

4. From eternity God's plan was that the glory of God's grace would reach its high point in the saving work of Jesus on the cross.

We see this in the name that was already on the book of the redeemed before the creation of the world. Before there was any human sin to die for, God planned that his Son be slain for sinners. We know this because of the name given to the book of life before creation. "Everyone [will worship the beast] whose name has not been written before the foundation of the world in *the book of life of the Lamb who was slain*" (Revelation 13:8).

The name of the book before creation was "the book of life of the Lamb who was slain." The plan was glory. The plan was grace. The plan was Christ. And the plan was death. And that death for sinners like us is the heart of the gospel, which is why in 2 Corinthians 4:4 Paul calls it "the gospel of the glory of Christ."

5. Therefore, the ultimate purpose of creating and guiding and sustaining this world—this history—is the praise of the glory of the grace of God in the crucifixion of his Son for sinners.

This is why Revelation 5:3, 9 shows that for all eternity we will sing "the song of the Lamb." We will say with white-hot admiration and praise, "Worthy are you to take the scroll and to open its seals, *for you were slain*, and by your blood you ransomed people for God from every tribe and language and people and nation" (Revelation 5:9). We will praise ten thousand things about our Savior. But we will not say anything more glorious than: You were slain… and ransomed millions.

So we ask in conclusion: "Why did God create the world?" And we answer with the Scriptures: God created the world for his glory. God did not create out of need. He did not create the world out of a deficiency that needed to be made up. He was not lonely. He was supremely happy in the fellowship of the Trinity—Father, Son, and Holy Spirit. He created the world to put his glory on display that his people might know him, and love him, and show him.

And why did he create a world that would become like this world? A world that fell into sin? A world that exchanged his glory for the glory of images? Why would he permit and guide and sustain such a world? And we answer: for the praise of the glory of the grace of God displayed supremely in the death of Jesus.

2.6 Four Questions About Your Life

The ultimate reason for all things is the communication of the glory of God's grace for the happy praise of a redeemed multitude from every people and tongue and tribe and nation. All things are created and guided and sustained for the glory of God, which reaches its apex in the glory of his grace, which shines most brightly and the glory of

Christ, which comes to focus most clearly in the glory of the cross.

So I ask:

- Is the glory of God the brightest treasure on the horizon of your future? Paul expressed the Christian heart in Romans 5:2, "We rejoice in hope of the glory of God."
- Is the glory of grace the sweetest news to your guilty soul?
- Is the glory of Christ in your life the present, personal embodiment of the grace of God?
- Is the glory of the cross the saddest and happiest beauty to your redeemed soul?

B. MORE ABOUT THE GLORY OF GOD

Seven Examples of God's Commitment to His Name

What does it mean that God has pleasure in his name?

It means that God has pleasure in his own perfections, in his own glory. The name of God in Scripture often means virtually the same thing as God's glorious, excellent character.

But it often means something slightly different, namely, the glory of God gone public. In other words, the name of God often refers to his reputation, his fame, his renown. This is the way we use the word "name" when we say someone is making a name for himself. Or we sometimes say, that's a "name" brand. We mean a brand with a reputation.

This is what I think Samuel means in 1 Samuel

12:22 when he says that God made Israel a people "for himself" and that he would not cast Israel off "for his great name's sake."

Let me point you to some other passages that bring out this idea of God's reputation or fame or renown.

1. God's Waistcloth

In Jeremiah 13:11 God describes Israel as a waistcloth that had been chosen to highlight God's glory, but had been found unusable.

> *For as the waistcloth clings to the loins of a man, so I made the whole house of Israel and the whole house of Judah cling to me, says the Lord, that they might be for me a people, a name, a praise, and a glory, but they would not listen.*

Why was Israel chosen and made the garment of God? That it might be a "name, a praise, and a glory." The words "praise" and "glory" in this context tell us that "name" means "renown" or "reputation." God chose Israel so that the people would make a reputation for him.

2. David's Teaching

David teaches the same thing in one of his prayers in 2 Samuel 7:23. He says that what sets Israel apart from all the other peoples is that God has dealt with them in such a way as to make a name for himself.

What other nation on earth is like thy people Israel, whom God went to redeem to be his people, making himself a name, and doing for them great and terrible things, by driving out before his people a nation and its gods?

In other words, when God went to redeem his people in Egypt and then bring them through the wilderness and into the promised land, he was not just favoring the people, he was acting, as Samuel says, for his own great name's sake (1 Samuel 12:22); or, as David says, he was making himself a name—a reputation.

3. The Point of the Exodus

Let's go back to the Exodus for a moment. This is where God really formed a people for himself. For the rest of her existence Israel has looked back to the exodus as the key event in her history. So in the exodus we can see what God is up to in choosing a people to himself.

In Exodus 9:16 God speaks to Pharaoh a word that lets him and us know why God is drawing out the deliverance to ten plagues instead of making short work of it in one swift catastrophe. This text is so crucial that Paul quotes it in Romans 9:17 to sum up God's purpose in the exodus. God says to Pharaoh, "But for this purpose have I let you live, to show you my power, so that my name may be declared throughout all the earth."

The point of the exodus was to make a worldwide reputation for God. The point of the ten plagues and miraculous Red Sea crossing was to demonstrate the incredible power of God on behalf of his freely chosen people, with the aim that this reputation, this name, would be declared throughout the whole world. God has great pleasure in his reputation.

4. The Testimony of Isaiah

Did the later prophets and poets of Israel interpret the Exodus that way? Yes, they did.

Isaiah says that God's aim in the exodus was to make for himself an everlasting name. He described God as the one "who caused his glorious arm to go at the right hand of Moses, who divided the waters before them to make for himself an everlasting name, who led them through the depths. Like a horse in the desert, they did not stumble. Like cattle that go down into the valley, the Spirit of the Lord gave them rest. So thou didst lead thy people, to make for thyself a glorious name" (Isaiah 63:12–14).

So when God showed his power to deliver his people from Egypt through the Red Sea, he had his sights on eternity and the everlasting reputation that he would win for himself in those days.

5. The Teaching of the Psalms

Psalm 106:7–8 teaches the same thing:

> *Our fathers, when they were in Egypt, did not consider thy wonderful works; they did not remember the abundance of thy steadfast love, but rebelled against the Most High at the Red Sea. Yet he saved them for his name's sake, that he might make known his mighty power.*

Do you see the same gospel logic at work here that we saw in our text of 1 Samuel 12:22? There the sinful people had chosen a king and angered God. But God does not cast them off. Why? For his great name's sake. Here it says that the sinful people had rebelled against God at the Red Sea and failed to consider his love. Yet he saved them with tremendous power. Why? Same answer: for his name's sake, to make known his mighty power.

Do you see that God's first love is his name and not his people? And because it is, there is hope for his sinful people. Do you see why the God-centeredness of God is the ground of the gospel?

6. Joshua's Prayer

Take Joshua as another example of someone who understood this God-centered gospel logic and put it to use like Moses did (Deuteronomy 9:27–29; Numbers 14:13–16) to plead for God's sinful people. In Joshua 7 Israel has crossed the Jordan and entered the promised land and defeated Jericho. But now they have been defeated at Ai and Joshua is stunned. He goes to the Lord in one of the most desperate prayers in all the Bible.

> *O Lord, what can I say, when Israel has turned their backs before their enemies! For the Canaanites and all the inhabitants of the land will hear of it, and will surround us, and cut off our name from the earth; and what wilt thou do for thy great name?*
> —Joshua 7:8–9

Do you cry for mercy on the basis of God's love for his name? The great ground of hope in all the God-centered servants of the Lord has always been the impossibility that God would let his great name be dishonored among the nations. It was inconceivable. This was bedrock confidence. Other things change but not this—not the commitment of God to his name.

7. Ezekiel's Witness in Exile

But what, then, are we to make of the fact that eventually Israel proved to be so rebellious that she was indeed given into the hands of her enemies in the Babylonian captivity during the time of Ezekiel? How does a God-centered prophet like Ezekiel handle this terrible setback for the reputation of God?

Listen to the word of the Lord that came to him in Ezekiel 36:20–23. This is God's answer to the captivity of his people which he himself had brought about:

> *But when they came to the nations, wherever they came, they profaned my holy name, in that men said of them, "These are the people of the Lord, and yet they had to go out of his land." But I had concern for my holy name, which the house of Israel caused to be profaned among the nations to which they came. Therefore say to the house of Israel, Thus says the Lord God: it is not for your sake, O house of Israel, that I am about to act, but for the sake of my holy name, which you have profaned among the nations to which you came. And I will vindicate the holiness of my great name, which has been profaned among the nations, which you have profaned among them; and the nations will know that I am the Lord, says the Lord God, when through you I vindicate my holiness before their eyes.*

In other words, when every other hope was gone and the people lay under the judgment of God himself because of their own sin, one hope remained—and it will always remain—that God has an indomitable delight in the worth of his own reputation and will not suffer it to be trodden down for long.

3. CHRISTIAN HEDONISM

I want you to know, brothers, that what has happened to me has really served to advance the gospel, [13] so that it has become known throughout the whole imperial guard and to all the rest that my imprisonment is for Christ. [14] And most of the brothers, having become confident in the Lord by my imprisonment, are much more bold to speak the word without fear. [15] Some indeed preach Christ from envy and rivalry, but others from good will. [16] The latter do it out of love, knowing that I am put here for the defense of the gospel. [17] The former proclaim Christ out of selfish ambition, not sincerely but thinking to afflict me in my imprisonment. [18] What then? Only that in every way, whether in pretense or in truth, Christ is proclaimed, and in that I rejoice.

Yes, and I will rejoice, [19] for I know that through your prayers and the help of the Spirit of Jesus Christ this will turn out for my deliverance, [20] as it is my eager expectation and hope that I will not be at all ashamed, but that with full courage now as always Christ will be honored in my body, whether by life or by death. [21] For to me to live is Christ, and to die is gain. [22] If I am to live in the flesh, that means fruitful labor for me. Yet which I shall choose I cannot tell. [23] I am hard pressed between the two. My desire is to depart and be with Christ, for that is far better. [24] But to remain in the flesh is more necessary on your account. [25] Convinced of this, I know that I will remain and continue with you all, for your progress and joy in the faith, [26] so that in me you may have ample cause to glory in Christ Jesus, because of my coming to you again. —Philippians 1:12–26

Let me be clear from the outset that Bethlehem has not been built around a slogan or a label. The term "Christian Hedonism" is not in any of this church's official documents. It's not in our constitution, or our church covenant, or our Elder Affirmation of Faith, or Values booklet, or our Ten Dimensions of Church Life. It's catchy, it's controversial, it's not in the Bible, and you don't need to like it just because I do.

So the point of this chapter is not at all to push a label or a slogan. The point is to talk about the massive and pervasive biblical truth that some of us love to call Christian Hedonism.

So this chapter is packed with some of the juiciest, most wonderful things that I love to know and experience. We need to get to work. Here's the outline:

- First, there's a problem that needs be solved because of Chapter Two on the glory of God.
- Second, Christian Hedonism is the biblical solution to that problem.
- C.S. Lewis and the apostle Paul give the basis for that solution.
- Fourth, this solution—Christian Hedonism—changes everything in your life, which I try to show in eleven examples.

3.1 Is God's Self-Promotion Loveless?

In Chapter 2, I asked, "Why did God create the world?" and answered: "God created this world *for the praise of the glory of his grace displayed supremely in the death of Jesus*." The problem is that, at the heart of that answer is God's self-promotion. God created the world for his own praise. For his own glory.

Oprah Winfrey, Brad Pitt, the early C.S. Lewis, Eric Reece, and Michael Prowse, among others, all walk away from such a God. They stumble over God's self-promotion.

- Oprah walked away from orthodox Christianity when she was about 27 because of the biblical teaching that God is jealous—he demands that he and no one else get our highest allegiance and affection. It didn't sound loving to her.
- Brad Pitt turned away from his boyhood faith, he says, because God says, "You have to say that I'm the best.... It seemed to be about ego."

- C.S. Lewis, before he became a Christian, complained that God's demand to be praised sounded like "a vain woman who wants compliments."
- Erik Reece, the writer of *An American Gospel*, rejected the Jesus of the Gospels because only an egomaniac would demand that we love him more than we love our parents and children.
- And Michael Prowse, columnist for the *London Financial Times*, turned away because only "tyrants, puffed up with pride, crave adulation."

So people see this as a problem—that God created the world for his own praise. They think such self-exaltation would be immoral and loveless. That may be how you feel.

3.2 Our Greatest Exhilaration and God's Greatest Glorification

God is most glorified in you when you are most satisfied in him. That's the shortest summary of what we mean by Christian Hedonism. If that is true, then there is no conflict between your greatest exhilaration and God's greatest glorification.

In fact, not only is there no conflict between your happiness and God's glory, but his glory shines in your happiness, when your happiness is in him. And since God is the source of greatest happiness, and since he is the greatest treasure in the world, and since his glory is the most satisfying gift he could possibly give us, therefore it is the kindest, most loving thing he could possibly do—to reveal himself, and magnify himself and vindicate himself for our everlasting enjoyment. "In your presence there is fullness of joy; at your right hand are pleasures forevermore" (Psalm 16:11).

God is the one being for whom self-exaltation is the most loving act, because he is exalting for us what alone can satisfy us fully and forever. If we exalt ourselves, we are not loving, because we distract people from the one Person who can make them happy forever—God. But if God exalts himself, he draws attention to the one Person who can make us happy forever—himself. He is not an egomaniac. He is an infinitely glorious, all-satisfying God, offering us everlasting and supreme joy in himself.

That's the solution to our problem.

› No Oprah, if God were not jealous for all your affections, he would be indifferent to your final misery.

› No Brad Pitt, if God didn't demand that you see him as the best, he wouldn't care about your supreme happiness.

› No Mr. Lewis, God is not vain in demanding your praise. This is his highest virtue, and your highest joy.

› No, Erik Reece, if Jesus didn't lay claim on greater love than your children do, he would be selling your heart to what cannot satisfy forever.

› No, Michael Prowse, God does not crave your adulation, he offers it as your greatest pleasure.

God is most glorified in you when you are most satisfied in him. God's design to pursue his own glory turns out to be love. And our duty to pursue God's glory turns out to be a quest for joy. That's the solution to the problem of God's self-exaltation.

3.3 The Realistic, Biblical Basis for Christian Hedonism

C.S. Lewis saw the basis in human experience. The apostle Paul shows it in his letter to the Philippians. Here is the great discovery as I first found it in Lewis's book, *Reflections on the Psalms*. He is discovering why God's demand for our praise is not vain.

> *The most obvious fact about praise—whether of God or any thing—strangely escaped me. I thought of it in terms of compliment, approval, or the giving of honor. I had never noticed that all enjoyment spontaneously overflows into praise unless... shyness or the fear of boring others is deliberately brought in to check it. The world rings with praise—lovers praising their mistresses, readers their favorite poet, walkers praising the countryside, players praising their favorite game—praise of weather, wines, dishes, actors, motors, horses, colleges, countries, historical personages, children, flowers, mountains, rare stamps, rare beetles, even sometimes politicians or scholars. I had not noticed how the humblest, and at the same time most balanced and capacious, minds, praised most, while the cranks, misfits and malcontents praised least....*
>
> *I had not noticed either that just as men spontaneously praise whatever they value, so they spontaneously urge us to join them in praising it: "Isn't she lovely? Wasn't it glorious? Don't you think that magnificent?" The Psalmists in telling everyone to praise God are doing*

> *what all men do when they speak of what they care about. My whole, more general, difficulty about the praise of God depended on my absurdly denying to us, as regards the supremely Valuable, what we delight to do, what indeed we can't help doing, about everything else we value.*
>
> *I think we delight to praise what we enjoy because the praise not merely expresses but completes the enjoyment; it is it's appointed consummation. It is not out of compliment that lovers keep on telling one another how beautiful they are; the delight is incomplete till it is expressed.* (C.S. Lewis, *Reflections on the Psalms* [New York: Harcourt, Brace and World, 1958], 93–95.)

There it was. God's relentless command that we see him as glorious and praise him is a command that we settle for nothing less than the completion of our joy in him. Praise is not just the expression, but the consummation, of our joy in what is supremely enjoyable, namely, God. In *his* presence is fullness of joy; at *his* right hand are pleasures forevermore (Psalm 16:11). In demanding our praise, he is demanding the completion of our pleasure. God is most glorified in us when we are most satisfied in him.

That Christ Be Seen As Great

And that is what we find in Philippians 1:20–21.

> *It is my eager expectation and hope that I will not be at all ashamed, but that with full courage now as always Christ will be honored* [magnified—to cause

to be seen as great] *in my body, whether by life or by death. For to me to live is Christ, and to die is gain.*

Paul says that his great passion in life—I hope it's your great passion in life—is that in this life Christ be seen as great—supremely great. That is why God created us and saved us—to make Christ look like what he really is—supremely great.

Now the relationship between verse 20 and 21 is the key to seeing how Paul thinks that happens. It's going to happen, Paul says—Christ is going to be magnified in my body by life or death—"because to me to live is Christ and to die is gain" (verse 21). Notice that "life" in verse 20 corresponds to "live" in verse 21 and "death" in verse 20 corresponds to "die" in verse 21. So Paul is explaining in both cases—life and death—how Christ is going to look great.

He will look great in my *life* because "for me to *live* is Christ." He explains in Philippians 3:8, "I count everything as loss because of the surpassing worth of knowing Christ Jesus my Lord." So Christ is more precious, more valuable, more satisfying than all that life on this earth can give. "I count everything as loss because of the surpassing worth of knowing Christ Jesus my Lord."

This is what he means when he says in Philippians 1:21, "To me to live is Christ." And *that* he says is how his life magnifies Christ—makes him look great. Christ is most magnified in Paul's life when Paul, in his life, is most satisfied in Christ. That's the plain teaching of these two texts.

When Our Death Is Gain

And it gets even plainer when you consider the death half of Philippians 1:20–21. Christ will be magnified in my body by death, "because to me to die is gain" (verse 21). Why would death be gain? The answer is at the end of verse 23: "My desire is to depart and be with Christ, for that is far better." Death is gain because it means a greater closeness of being with Christ. Death is "to depart and be with Christ."

This is why Paul says in verse 21 that to die is gain. You add up all the losses that death will cost you (your family, your job, your dream retirement, the friends you leave behind, your favorite bodily pleasures)—you add up all these losses, and then you replace them only with death and Christ—if when you do that you joyfully say, *gain*!, then Christ is magnified in your dying. Christ is most magnified in your death, when you are so satisfied in Christ, that losing everything and getting only Christ is called gain.

Or to sum up both halves of the verse: *Christ is glorified in you when he is more precious to you than all that life can give or death can take.*

3.4 The Centrality of the Cross in Christian Hedonism

That's the biblical basis for Christian Hedonism: God is most glorified in us when we are most satisfied in him.

And this really was already implicit in Chapter Two on the glory of God. God created the world *for the praise of the glory of his grace displayed supremely in the death of Jesus.* Which means that the pursuit of his own praise reaches its climax at the place where it does us the most good, the cross. At the cross God upholds his glory and provides our forgiveness. At the cross God vindicates his own honor and secures our happiness. At the cross God magnifies his own worth and satisfies our soul.

In the greatest act of history, Christ made it come true for undeserving sinners that God could be most glorified in us by our being most satisfied in him.

3.5 11 Illustrations of How Christian Hedonism Changes Everything

1. Death

We've just seen how it changes death. If you want to make Christ look great in your dying, there is no big performance or achievement or heroic sacrifice. There is simply a childlike laying yourself into the arms of the one who makes the loss of everything gain.

2. Conversion

Christian Hedonism changes how we think about conversion. Matthew 13:44: "The kingdom of heaven is like treasure hidden in a field, which a man found and covered up. Then in his joy he goes and sells all that he has and buys that field." Becoming a Christian not only means believing truth; it means finding a treasure. So evangelism becomes not only persuasion about truth but pointing people to a Treasure—that is more valuable than everything they have.

3. The Fight of Faith

Christian Hedonism changes "the good fight of faith" (1 Timothy 6:12). John says in John 1:12, "To all who *received* Jesus, who *believed* in his name, he gave the right to become children of God" (John 1:12). Believing Jesus is receiving him. As what? As the infinitely valuable Treasure that he is. Faith is seeing and savoring this Treasure. And so the fight of faith is a fight for joy in Jesus. A fight to see and savor Jesus is more precious than anything in the world. Because this savoring shows him to be supremely valuable.

4. Combating Evil

Christian Hedonism changes how we combat evil in our lives. Jeremiah 2:13 gives the Christian Hedonist definition of evil: "My people have committed two evils: they have forsaken me, the fountain of living waters, and hewed out cisterns for themselves, broken cisterns that can hold no water." Evil is the suicidal preference for the empty wells of the world over the living waters of God's fellowship. We fight evil by the pursuit of the fullest satisfaction in the river of God's delights (Psalm 36:8).

5. What Hell Is

Christian Hedonism changes how we think of hell. Since the way to be saved and go to heaven is to embrace Jesus as your source of greatest joy, hell is a place of suffering, a place of eternal unhappiness, prepared for people who refuse to be happy in the triune God.

6. Self-Denial

Christian Hedonism changes the way we think about self-denial. Self-denial really is there in the teachings of Jesus, "If anyone would come after me, let him deny himself and take up his cross and follow me" (Mark 8:34). But now the meaning becomes,

› Deny yourself the wealth of the world so you can have the wealth of being with Christ.

› Deny yourself the fame of the world to have the joy of God's approval.

› Deny yourself the security and safety of the world to have the solid, secure fellowship of Jesus.

› Deny yourself the short, unsatisfying pleasures of the world so that you can have fullness of joy and pleasures forevermore at God's right hand.

Which means there is no such thing as ultimate self-denial, because to live is Christ and to die is gain.

7. Money

Christian Hedonism changes the way we think about handling our money and the act of giving. Acts 20:35: "It is more blessed to give than to receive." 2 Corinthians 9:7: "Each one must give as he has decided in his heart, not reluctantly or under compulsion, for God loves a cheerful giver." The motive to be a generous person is that it expresses and expands our joy in God. And the pursuit of deepest joy is the pursuit of giving not getting.

8. Corporate Worship

Christian Hedonism changes the way we do corporate worship. Corporate worship is the collective act of glorifying God. But God is glorified in that service when the people are satisfied in him. Therefore, the worship leaders—musicians and preachers—see their task primarily as breaking open a fountain of living water and spreading a feast of rich food. The task of the worshippers is to drink and eat and say a satisfied "Ahhh." Because God is most glorified in those worshippers when they are most satisfied in him.

9. Disability and Weakness

Christian Hedonism changes the way we experience disability and weakness. Stunningly, paradoxically, Jesus says to the weak and thorn-pierced Paul, "My grace is sufficient for you, for my power is made perfect in weakness." To which Paul responds, "Therefore I will boast all the more gladly [yes this is the voice of the thorn-pierced Christian Hedonist] of my weaknesses, so that the power of Christ may rest upon me" (2 Corinthians 12:9).

10. Love

Christian Hedonism changes the meaning of love. Paul describes the love of the Macedonians like this: "In a severe test of affliction, their *abundance of joy* and their extreme poverty have overflowed in a wealth of generosity on their part" (2 Corinthians 8:2). In verse 8, Paul calls this "love." "Abundant joy" in "severe affliction" and "extreme poverty" overflowed in loving generosity. Still poor. Still afflicted. But so full of joy it overflowed in love. So Christian Hedonism defines love as the overflow (or the expansion) of joy in God that meets the needs of others.

11. Ministry

Christian Hedonism changes the meaning of ministry. What is the ministry aim of the great apostle Paul? 2 Corinthians 1:24, "Not that we lord it over your faith, but we are workers with you for your joy, for you stand firm in your faith." All ministry should be one way or the other a working with others for their joy.

That's why God created you. That's why Christ died for you. That's why we serve you as your pastors. And that is why I have preached this message. We are workers with you for your joy in God. Because God is most glorified in you when you are most satisfied in him.

C. MORE ABOUT CHRISTIAN HEDONISM

Eight Reasons to Pursue Your Satisfaction in God

The *implications* of Christian Hedonism are pervasive. One of the biggest implications is that we should, therefore, pursue our joy in God. *Should*! Not *may*. The main business of our hearts is maximizing our satisfaction in God. *Not* our satisfaction in his gifts, no matter how good, but in him.

Here are eight biblical reasons to pursue your greatest and longest satisfaction in God.

1. We are commanded to pursue satisfaction.

Psalm 100:2: "Serve the Lord with gladness!"
Philippians 4:4: "Rejoice in the Lord always."
Psalm 37:4: "Delight yourself in the Lord."

2. We are threatened if we don't pursue satisfaction in God.

Deuteronomy 28:47–48: "Because you did not serve the Lord your God with joyfulness and gladness of heart... therefore you shall serve your enemies."

3. The nature of faith teaches the pursuit of satisfaction in God.

Hebrews 11:6: "Without faith it is impossible to please him, for whoever would draw near to God must believe that he exists and that he rewards those who seek him."

4. The nature of evil teaches the pursuit of satisfaction in God.

Jeremiah 2:12–13: "Be appalled, O heavens, at this; be shocked, be utterly desolate, declares the Lord, for my people have committed two evils: they have forsaken me, the fountain of living waters, and hewed out cisterns for themselves, broken cisterns that can hold no water."

5. The nature of conversion teaches the pursuit of satisfaction in God.

Matthew 13:44: "The kingdom of heaven is like treasure

hidden in a field, which a man found and covered up. Then *in his joy* he goes and sells all that he has and buys that field."

6. The call for self-denial teaches the pursuit of satisfaction in God.

Mark 8:34–36: "If anyone would come after me, let him deny himself and take up his cross and follow me. For whoever would save his life will lose it, but whoever loses his life for my sake and the gospel's *will save it*. For what does it profit a man to gain the whole world and forfeit his soul?"

7. The demand to love people teaches the pursuit of satisfaction in God.

Hebrews 12:2: "For the joy that was set before him [Jesus] endured the cross."
Acts 20:35: "It is more blessed to give than to receive."

8. The demand to glorify God teaches the pursuit of satisfaction in God.

Philippians 1:20–21: "It is my eager expectation and hope that... Christ will be [glorified] in my body, whether by life or by death. For to me to live is Christ, and to die is gain (final and total satisfaction in *him*)."

Therefore, I invite you to join George Mueller, the great prayer warrior and lover of orphans, in saying, "I saw more clearly than ever, that the first great and primary business to which I ought to attend every day was, to have my soul happy in the Lord." In this way, we will be able to suffer the loss of all things in the sacrifices of love, and "count it all joy."

What About Self-Denial?

Someone may say, "How can you talk as if it is right to be motivated by a desire for our own good? How can you say, 'Make pleasure your aim,' when the Bible so clearly teaches we should deny ourselves and take up our cross?"

Well, I have good news for you, if you think that's what Jesus taught. Let's read the whole passage of Mark 8:34–36:

> *If anyone would come after me, let him deny himself and take up his cross and follow me. For whoever would save his life will lose it, but whoever loses his life for my sake and the gospel's will save it. For what does it profit a man to gain the whole world and forfeit his soul?*

The whole premise of this argument is hedonistic. Nobody wants to lose his life. There is no profit—no pleasure—in that. So here is how to save your life and have infinite joy—lose it in a life of love. Every sacrifice Jesus asks us to make, he asks us to make because he promises something vastly better. Self-denial? Sure: deny yourself the mud pie in the slum so you can have the day at the sea, as Lewis has said.

Jesus asked a rich young man once to deny himself, to sell everything he had, give it to the poor, and follow Jesus. Now what do you think should have motivated that man to sell all his goods? Some kind of disinterested benevolence? The Bible does not know any such thing.

Jesus told two parables to show what his motive should have been. Matthew 13:44–46: "The kingdom of heaven is like a treasure hidden in a field which a man found and covered up; then *in his joy* he goes and sells all that he has and buys that field." The rich young man should have sold all that he had because the prospect of following Jesus into the kingdom was so exciting and so joyful that all his possessions were no comparison." Again, the kingdom of heaven is like a merchant in search of fine pearls, who, on finding one pearl of great value, went and sold all that he had and bought it."

The only reason Jesus asks us to renounce our little plastic beads of money and vain ambition and sensual pleasures is because he has a real pearl for us.

There is no such thing as ultimate self-sacrifice in the kingdom of God. Even Jesus, whose love was purest at Calvary, "endured the cross," as Hebrews 12:2 says, "for the *joy* that was set before him." Christian hedonism is simply a fancy way of saying it is not the best when we do things under compulsion, for it is *cheerful* givers, joyful lovers, that the Lord seeks (2 Corinthians 9:7).

I conclude with a letter I wrote to one of my past students who disagreed with me on this. He wrote me a note and said, "I disagree with your position that love seeks or is motivated by its own pleasure... Are you familiar with Dorothy Day? She is a very old woman who has devoted her life to loving others, especially the poor, displaced and downtrodden. Her experience of loving when there was no joy has led her to say this: 'Love in action is a harsh and dreadful thing.'"

I wrote back the following response:

You say of Dorothy Day: "Her experience of loving the poor, displaced, downtrodden when there was no joy has led her to say this: 'Love in action is a harsh and dreadful thing.'" I will try to respond in two ways.

First, don't jump to the conclusion that there is no joy in things that are "harsh and dreadful." There are mountain climbers who have spent sleepless nights on the faces of cliffs, have lost fingers and toes in subzero temperatures, and have gone through horrible misery to reach a peak. They say it is "harsh and dreadful." But if you ask them why they do it, the answer will come back in various forms: there is an exhilaration in the soul that feels so good it is worth all the pain.

And if this is how it is with mountain climbing, cannot the same be true of love? Is it not rather an indictment of our own worldliness that we are more inclined to sense exhilaration at mountain climbing than at conquering the precipices of un-love in our own lives and in society?

Yes, love is often a "harsh and dreadful" thing, but I do not see how a person who cherishes what is good and admires Jesus can help but feel a sense of joyful exhilaration when (by grace) he is able to love another person.

Now let me approach Dorothy Day's situation in another way. Let's pretend I am one of the poor that she is trying to help at great cost to herself. I think a conversation might go like this:

Piper: Why are you doing this for me, Miss Day?

Day: Because I love you.

Piper: What do you mean, you love me? I don't have

anything to offer. I am not worth loving.

Day: Perhaps. But there are no application forms for my love. I learned that from Jesus. What I mean is I want to *help* you because Jesus has helped me so much.

Piper: So you are trying to satisfy your "wants?"

Day: I suppose so, if you want to put it like that. One of my deepest wants is to make you a happy and purposeful person.

Piper: Does it upset you that I *am* happier and that I feel more purposeful since you've come?

Day: Heavens no! What could make me happier!

Piper: So you really spend all these sleepless nights here for what makes you happy, don't you?

Day: If I say "yes" someone might misunderstand me. They might think I don't care for *you* at all, but only for myself.

Piper: But won't you say it at least for me?

Day: Yes, I'll say it for you: I work for what brings me the greatest joy: *your joy.*

Piper: Thank you. Now I know that you love me.

4. THE SOVEREIGNTY OF GOD

> *Remember this and stand firm, recall it to mind, you transgressors,* [9] *remember the former things of old; for I am God, and there is no other; I am God, and there is none like me,* [10] *declaring the end from the beginning and from ancient times things not yet done, saying, 'My counsel shall stand, and I will accomplish all my purpose,'* [11] *calling a bird of prey from the east, the man of my counsel from a far country. I have spoken, and I will bring it to pass; I have purposed, and I will do it.* —Isaiah 46:8–11

One of the most foundational of all the thirty-year theological trademarks is the priceless truth of the sovereignty of God. Let's go right to our text lest even from the beginning we import something here that does not come from the word of God. This matter is far too serious, and touches on so many painful realities, that we dare not trust ourselves here to come up with truth without being told by God himself.

In Isaiah 46:9 God says, "I am God, and there is no other; I am God, and there is none like me." So the issue in this text is the uniqueness of God among all the beings of the universe. He is in a class by himself. No one is like him. The issue is what it means to be God. When something is happening, or something is being said or thought, and God responds, "I am God!" (which is what he does in verse 9), the point is: You're acting like you don't know what it means for me to be God.

4.1 What It Means to Be God

God tells us what it means to be the one and only God. He tells us what's at the heart of his God-ness. Verse 10: *What it means for me to be God is that "I declare the end from the beginning and from ancient times things not yet done."*

Two statements: One, *I declare how things turn out long before they ever happen*. Second, *I declare not just natural events but human events*—doings, things that are not yet done. Verse 10: "I declare from ancient times things not yet done." *I know what these doings will be long before they are done*.

Now at this point you might say, "What we have here is the doctrine of God's foreknowledge, not the doctrine of his sovereignty." And that is right, so far. But in the next half of the verse God tells us *how* he foreknows the end and *how* he foreknows the things not yet done. Verse 10b: "I declare the end from the beginning and from ancient times things not yet done, saying, 'My counsel shall stand, and I will accomplish all my purpose.'" When he "declares" ahead of time what will be, here's how he "declares" it, or "says" it: "saying, 'My counsel shall stand, and I will accomplish all my purpose.'"

In other words, the way he declares his foreknowledge is by declaring his fore-counsel and his fore-purposing. When God declares the end long before it happens, what he says is: "My counsel shall stand." And when God declares things not yet done long before they are done, what he says is: "I will accomplish all my purpose."

Which means that the reason God knows the future is because he plans the future and accomplishes it. The future is the counsel of God being established. The future is the purpose of God being accomplished by God. Then, the next verse, verse 11b, gives a clear confirmation that this is what he means: "I have spoken, and *I will bring it to pass*; I have purposed, and *I will do it*." In other words, *the reason my predictions come true is because they are my purposes, and because I myself perform them.*

4.2 God Purposes All Things

God is not a fortuneteller, a soothsayer, a mere predictor. He doesn't have a crystal ball. He knows what's coming because he plans what's coming and he performs what he plans. Verse 10b: "My counsel shall stand, and I will accomplish all my purpose." He does not form purposes and wonder if someone else will take responsibility to make them happen. "I will accomplish all my purpose."

So, based on this text, here's what I mean by the sovereignty of God: God has the rightful authority, the freedom, the wisdom, and the power to bring about everything that he intends to happen. And therefore, everything he intends to come about does come about. Which means: God plans and governs all things.

When he says, "I will accomplish all my purpose," he means, "Nothing happens except what is my purpose." If something happened that God did not purpose to happen, he would say, "That's not what I purposed to happen."

And we would ask, "What did you purpose to happen?"

And he would say, "I purposed this other thing to happen which didn't happen."

To which we would all say, then, "But you said in Isaiah 46:10, 'I will accomplish all my purpose.'"

And he would say, "That's right."

Therefore, what God means in Isaiah 46:10 is that nothing has ever happened, or will ever happen that God did not purpose to happen. Or to put it positively: Everything that happened or will happen is purposed by God to happen.

Now if that seemed a little too complicated, let's do something simpler. Let's confirm this view of God's sovereignty by looking at some other passages of scripture.

4.3 A Straightforward Statement on Sovereignty

Before we look closer at some important passages of Scripture, let me refer to the *Bethlehem Baptist Church Elder Affirmation of Faith*. My exposition of this doctrine is not me expressing a private opinion. I'm simply expressing and supporting a doctrine to which all the elders of this church give their heartfelt affirmation.

> *3.1 We believe that God, from all eternity, in order to display the full extent of his glory for the eternal and ever-increasing enjoyment of all who love*

him, did, by the most wise and holy counsel of his will, freely and unchangeably ordain and foreknow whatever comes to pass.

3. 2 We believe that God upholds and governs all things—from galaxies to subatomic particles, from the forces of nature to the movements of nations, and from the public plans of politicians to the secret acts of solitary persons—all in accord with his eternal, all-wise purposes to glorify himself, yet in such a way that he never sins, nor ever condemns a person unjustly; but that his ordaining and governing all things is compatible with the moral accountability of all persons created in his image.

3. 3 We believe that God's election is an unconditional act of free grace which was given through his Son Christ Jesus before the world began. By this act God chose, before the foundation of the world, those who would be delivered from bondage to sin and brought to repentance and saving faith in his Son Christ Jesus.

So this is the way the sovereignty of God is expressed in our *Elder Affirmation of Faith*. Now, consider with me the extent of support for this in the Bible, and then some closing implications, and why it is so precious to us.

4.4 The Choice We All Face

The extent of God's sovereignty may be overwhelming for you. It is for me. And when we're confronted with this truth we all face a choice: will we turn from our objections and praise his power and grace, and bow with glad submission to the absolute sovereignty of God? Or will we stiffen our neck and resist him?

Will we see in the sovereignty of God our only hope for life in our deadness, our only hope for answers to our prayers, our only hope for success in our evangelism, our only hope for meaning in our suffering? Or will we insist that there is a better hope, or no hope? That's the question we will face.

Let it be said loud and clear that nothing you are about to read below, as paradoxical as it may seem to our finite minds, contradicts the real moral responsibility that humans and angels and demons have to do what God commands. God has given us a will. How we use it makes our eternal difference.

Let's divide God's sovereignty into his governing natural events on the one hand and human events on the other. In the first case he is governing physical processes. And in the second case he is governing human choices.

4.5 God's Sovereignty in the World Around Us

God is sovereign over what appear the most random acts in the world. Proverbs 16:33, "The lot is cast into the lap, but its every decision is from the Lord." In modern language we would say, "The dice are rolled on the table and every play is decided by God." There are no events so small that he does not rule for his purposes. "Are not two sparrows sold for a penny?" Jesus said, "And not one of them will fall to the ground apart from your Father. But even the hairs of your head are all numbered" (Matthew

10:29–30). Every role of the dice in Las Vegas, every tiny bird that falls dead in the thousand forests—all of this is God's command.

From worms in the ground to stars in the galaxies God governs the natural world. In the book of Jonah God commands a fish to swallow (1:17), God commands a plant to grow (4:6), and commands a worm to kill it (4:7). And far above the life of worms the stars take their place and hold their place at God's command: Isaiah 40:26, "Lift up your eyes on high and see: who created these? He who brings out their host by number, calling them all by name, by the greatness of his might, and because he is strong in power not one is missing." How much more, then, the natural events of this world—from weather to disasters to disease to disability to death.

Psalm 147:15–18, "He sends out his command to the earth; his word runs swiftly. He gives snow like wool; he scatters hoarfrost like ashes. He hurls down his crystals of ice like crumbs; who can stand before his cold? He sends out his word, and melts them; he makes his wind blow and the waters flow." Job 37:11–13, "He loads the thick cloud with moisture; the clouds scatter his lightning. They turn around and around by his guidance, to accomplish all that he commands them on the face of the habitable world. Whether for correction or for his land or for love, he causes it to happen."

4.6 God's Sovereignty in the Details

Snow and rain and cold and heat and wind are all the work of God. So when Jesus finds himself in the middle of a raging storm, he merely speaks, "Peace! Be still!" And the wind ceased, and there was a great calm (Mark 4:39). There is no wind, no storm, no hurricane, no cyclone, no typhoon, no monsoon, no tornado over which Jesus can say "Be still," and it will not obey. Which means, that if it blows, he intends for it to blow. "Does disaster come to a city, unless the Lord has done it?" (Amos 3:6). All Jesus had to do with Hurricane Sandy was say, "Be still," and there would have been no damage and no loss of life.

And what about the other sufferings of this life? "The Lord said to Moses, 'Who has made man's mouth? Who makes him mute, or deaf, or seeing, or blind? Is it not I, the Lord?'" (Exodus 4:11). And Peter said to the suffering saints in Asia Minor, "Let those who suffer according to God's will entrust their souls to a faithful Creator while doing good" (1 Peter 4:19). "It is better to suffer for doing good, if that should be God's will, than for doing evil" (1 Peter 3:17).

Whether we suffer from disability or from the evil of others God is the one who ultimately decides—and whether we live or die. Deuteronomy 32:39, "There is no god beside me; I kill and I make alive; I wound and I heal; and there is none that can deliver out of my hand." Or James 4:13–15, "Come now, you who say, 'Today or tomorrow we will go into such and such a town and spend a year there and trade and make a profit'—yet you do not know what tomorrow will bring. What is your life? For you are a mist that appears for a little time and then vanishes. Instead you ought to say, 'If the Lord wills, we will live and do this or that.'" Or as Job says, "Naked I came from my mother's womb, and naked shall I return. The

Lord gave, and the Lord has taken away; blessed be the name of the Lord" (Job 1:21).

The roll of the dice, the fall of a bird, the crawl of a worm, the movement of stars, the falling of snow, the blowing of wind, the loss of sight, the suffering of saints, and the death of all—these are included in the word of God: "I will accomplish all my purpose"—from the smallest to the greatest.

4.7 God's Sovereignty in Human Actions

When we turn from the natural world to consider the world of human actions and human choice, God's sovereignty is still amazingly extensive. You should vote in political elections—on the candidates and on the amendments. But let there be no man-exalting illusion as though mere human beings will be the decisive cause in any victory or loss. God alone will have that supreme role. "He changes times and seasons; he removes kings and sets up kings; ... the Most High rules the kingdom of men and gives it to whom he will" (Daniel 2:21; 4:17).

And whoever the next president is, he will not be sovereign. He will be governed. And we should pray for him that he would know this: "The king's heart is a stream of water in the hand of the Lord; he turns it wherever he will" (Proverbs 21:1). And when he engages in foreign affairs he will not be decisive. God will. "The Lord brings the counsel of the nations to nothing; he frustrates the plans of the peoples. The counsel of the Lord stands forever, the plans of his heart to all generations" (Psalm 33:10–11).

When nations came to do their absolute worst, namely the murder of the Son of God, Jesus Christ, they had not slipped out of God's control, but were doing his sweetest bidding at their worst moment: "Truly in this city there were gathered together against your holy servant Jesus, whom you anointed, both Herod and Pontius Pilate, along with the Gentiles and the peoples of Israel, to do *whatever your hand and your plan had predestined to take place*" (Acts 4:27–28). The worst sin that ever happened was in God's plan, and by that sin, sin died.

4.8 God's Sovereignty in Your Own Life

Our salvation was secured on Calvary under the sovereign hand of God. And, if you are a believer in Jesus, if you love him, you are a walking miracle. God granted you repentance (2 Timothy 2:24f). God drew you to Christ (John 6:44). God revealed the Son of God to you (Matthew 11:27). God gave you the gift of faith. "By grace you have been saved through faith. And this is not your own doing; it is the gift of God, not a result of works, so that no one may boast" (Ephesians 2:8–9). The sovereignty of God in our salvation excludes boasting.

There may have been a hundred horrible things in your life. But, if today, you are moved to treasure Christ as your Lord and Savior, you can write over every one of those horrors the words of Genesis 50:20: Satan, "you meant evil against me, but God meant it for good."

I conclude therefore with the words of Paul in Ephesians 1:11, "God works all things according to the counsel of his will." All things—from the roll of the dice, to the circuits of stars, to the rise of presidents, to the death of Jesus, to the gift of repentance and faith.

4.9 Seven Exhortations for How We Live Because God Is Sovereign

What does God's sovereignty mean for our lives? Why is this precious to us? I will state these reasons as exhortations. Because God is sovereign:

1. Let us stand in awe of the sovereign authority and freedom and wisdom and power of God.
2. And let us never trifle with life as though it were a small or light affair.
3. Let us marvel at our own salvation—that God bought it and wrought it with sovereign power, and we are not our own.
4. Let us groan over the God-belittling man-centeredness of our culture and much of the church.
5. Let us be bold at the throne of grace, knowing that our prayers for the most difficult things can be answered. Nothing is too hard for God.
6. Let us rejoice that our evangelism will not be in vain because there is no sinner so hard the sovereign grace of God cannot break through.
7. Let us be thrilled and calm in these days of great upheaval because victory belongs to God, and no purposes that he wills to accomplish can be stopped.

D. MORE ABOUT GOD'S SOVEREIGNTY

The Preciousness of God's Sovereignty in Our Pain

The deep inner-workings of the Christian soul are not possible without the sovereignty of God. The reason is because the strength of hope and peace and joy and contentment and gladness and satisfaction and delight in God that sustain the soul in sorrows of life-long disappointment are rooted in the confidence that God has the authority, the freedom, the wisdom, and the power to accomplish all the good he has promised to do for his embattled children.

In other words, no obstacle in nature, no obstacle in Satan, no obstacle in the failures and sins of man can stop God from making all my experiences, all my brokenness, all my adversaries, serve my eternal wholeness and joy. If you listen carefully to that, you can hear that my exuberance for God's sovereignty rests not mainly on his causality in the past but mainly on his powerful capacities in the future. In other words, the main reason God's sovereignty is precious is that he has power to fulfill impossible promises to me in my seemingly hopeless condition. His ruling the past, including my brokenness, is simply a pre-condition of this hope-filled power. So let me give a very brief glimpse at this sovereignty.

The Whole World in His Hands

One of the most sweeping and foundational texts on the sovereignty of God deals directly with disabilities. In Exodus 4:11 God answers Moses's fear that his eloquence is insufficient for the task, "The Lord said to him, 'Who has made man's mouth? Who makes him mute, or deaf, or seeing, or blind? Is it not I, the Lord?'" Disability of speech impediments, disability of deafness, disability of blindness—all of these are in God's hands to give and to remove.

To which we may respond by asking: "What about natural causes? What about Satan? What about the sins of others against us, or even our own sin?" And the answer is that these are real, but that none is finally decisive. If any of these play a role in our disability—and they do—they do so within God's sovereign plan.

For example, Romans 8:22–23 makes it clear that our physical groaning with disease and disability is owing to the fact that our bodies share in the fall of all nature into futility.

> *We know that the whole creation has been groaning together in the pains of childbirth until now. And not only the creation, but we ourselves, who have the firstfruits of the Spirit, groan inwardly as we wait eagerly for adoption as sons, the redemption of our bodies.*

So one cause of our physical and mental brokenness is that we share with the whole creation in its subjection to futility. But that creation is under the detailed governance of God. The Bible tells us that the roll of the dice, the fall of a bird, the crawl of a worm, the movement of stars, the fall of snow, the blowing of wind, the loss of sight, the suffering of saints, and the death of every person are included in the word of God: "I will accomplish all my purpose" (Isaiah 46:10). And in the word "He works all things according to the counsel of his will" (Ephesians 1:11).

So yes, there are natural causes for our disabilities, but none of these natural causes is ultimate, none is finally decisive. God is.

Even Satan Is Under God's Governance

So it is with Satan. He is real. And he is involved in damaging and hurting God's people, including physically and mentally (Acts 10:38). But he is under God's governance. In the book of Job Satan must come to God for permission to hurt Job (1:12; 2:6). And when he has done his work, striking Job with loathsome sores (2:7), Job says, "Shall we receive good *from God*, and shall we not receive evil?" (2:10). And the inspired author of the book says, "In all this Job did not sin with his lips" (2:10). And later said that Job was comforted "for all the evil that *the Lord had brought upon him*" (42:11).

So, yes, Satan is real and no doubt has a hand in causing many diseases and disabilities. But he can do nothing without God's permission. And what God foreknows and permits, he plans. And what he plans for his children is always for their good.

Sovereign Over Sin and Its Effects

And so it is with sins. We may smoke our way into emphysema, or we may lose a leg because a drunk driver crashes into us. But neither our sins nor the sins of another are finally decisive in what happens to us. God is. And the Christian may write over every attack of nature, Satan, or sin the words of Genesis 50:20, "As for you, you meant evil against me, but God meant it for good."

And the reason we can say this, even though we are undeserving sinners, is that God said it first over all the sins that brought his son to the cross for us. Herod, Pilate, cruel soldiers, shouting crowds—you meant my son's execution for evil, but I meant it for good (Acts 4:27–28). That's the foundation of all the good God promises in and through our disabilities.

And the good God has in mind for his children has an immeasurable number of layers. He means it for greater faith: 2 Corinthians 1:9, "We felt that we had received the sentence of death. But that was to make us *rely not on ourselves but on God who raises the dead*." He means it for greater righteousness: Hebrews 12:11, "For the moment all discipline seems painful rather than pleasant, but later it yields the peaceful fruit of righteousness." He means it for greater hope: Romans 5:3–4, "We rejoice in our sufferings, knowing that suffering produces endurance, and endurance produces character, and character produces hope." He means it for the greater experience of the glory of God: 2 Corinthians 4:17, "For this light momentary affliction is preparing for us an eternal weight of glory beyond all comparison."

"*You*, Satan, *you*, natural causes, *you*, sinner—you all meant my disability for evil, but God meant it for good—the good of greater faith, the good of greater righteousness, the good of greater hope, the good of greater glory." Or, as John 9:3 says, don't even consider secondary causes: "It was not that this man sinned, or his parents, but that the works of God might be displayed in him."

Only God Is Decisive

Though nature and Satan and sin may have a hand in disability, and should be resisted with prayer and truth and medicine, nevertheless, they are not decisive. God is.

And therein lies, for us, not mainly a theological problem with the past, but an invincible hope for the future. If God is sovereign then nothing is too hard for him. And by the blood of his Son he has promised infallibly: *I will meet all your needs according to my riches in glory in Christ Jesus* (Philippians 4:19). *My power will be made perfect in weakness* (2 Corinthians 12:9). *I will strengthen you and help you and hold you up with my righteous right hand* (Isaiah 41:10). *I will never leave you nor forsake you* (Hebrews 13:5). *I will not let any testing befall you for which I do not give you grace to bear* (1 Corinthians 10:13). *And I will take the sting away from your death with the blood of my son* (1 Corinthians 15:55f). *And I will raise you from the dead imperishable* (1 Corinthians 15:52), *and I will transform your lowly body to be like my glorious body, by the power that enables me even to subject all things to myself* (Philippians 3:21). *And I will do this without fail because I am absolutely sovereign over everything and therefore, I can do all things, and no purpose of mine can be thwarted* (Job 42:2).

This is the foundation of our hope and the key to the inner-workings of the Christian soul.

5. THE GOSPEL OF GOD IN CHRIST

Therefore, since we have been justified by faith,
we have peace with God through our Lord Jesus
Christ. 2 *Through him we have also obtained access*
by faith into this grace in which we stand, and
we rejoice in hope of the glory of God. 3 *Not only*
that, but we rejoice in our sufferings, knowing that
suffering produces endurance, 4 *and endurance*
produces character, and character produces
hope, 5 *and hope does not put us to shame, because*
God's love has been poured into our hearts through
the Holy Spirit who has been given to us. 6 *For while*
we were still weak, at the right time Christ died for
the ungodly. 7 *For one will scarcely die for a righteous*
person—though perhaps for a good person one would
dare even to die— 8 *but God shows his love for us*
in that while we were still sinners, Christ died for
us. 9 *Since, therefore, we have now been justified by*
his blood, much more shall we be saved by him from

the wrath of God. [10] *For if while we were enemies we were reconciled to God by the death of his Son, much more, now that we are reconciled, shall we be saved by his life.* [11] *More than that, we also rejoice in God through our Lord Jesus Christ, through whom we have now received reconciliation.* —Romans 5:1–11

5.1 What Is a Theological "Trademark?"

When you read about these "thirty-year theological trademarks" don't think niche branding. Don't think "thirty-year *exclusives.*" I don't even like the word "distinctives." It seems to connote a desire to be doctrinally different from others. Our mindset is exactly the opposite. We're suspicious of being different from the historic teachings of the church. The last thing we want to preach is new doctrines exclusive to us. When we say "trademarks" we mean truths that are defining and shaping and precious. We don't mean views that we've come up with and that set us off from the rest of the church of Christ. We don't want to be set off. We want to be arm in arm with millions of faithful followers of God's word. Truth does divide. But it also unites. And it is the uniting power of truth that we delight in most.

So we are always testing our interpretations of the Bible by looking back into church history. If we can't find our interpretations there, we would be very slow to preach them in this pulpit. Cults and sects are born in the minds of leaders who crave to be different. Jehovah's Witnesses, Mormons, the Unification Church, Christian Science—these were born in the minds of teachers who wanted new revelations and interpretations, and found them. They were restless with the limitation of the Bible and its historic understandings.

There is a lot of healthy and warranted warning these days about historical hero worship. Warnings about inordinate and uncritical admiration and imitation of historical teachers like Augustine, Aquinas, Calvin, Luther, the Puritans, Edwards, Wesley, Spurgeon, Barth, Chesterton, Lewis, etc. But we should be careful not to overdo this criticism. People with great historical heroes tend not to think of themselves as heroes. They're too busy learning from them. Which means that, for all its dangers, admiring a great line of historical heroes will at least keep you from starting a sect.

Our instincts are much more in that direction. Our thirty-year theological trademarks are not new, they're not distinctive to us, they are not a niche, they are not exclusives, they are not eccentric. They all have wide foundations in the Bible and deep roots in the history of God's people. And if any of them ever deserved to be guarded from the distortion of novelty it is this trademark, namely the gospel of Jesus Christ.

The key phrase is that God in Christ is the price and the prize of the gospel. *The prize of the gospel is the Person who paid the price, God in Christ.*

In other words, the gospel is the good news that God in Christ paid the price of suffering, so that we could have the prize of enjoying him forever. *God paid the price of his Son to give us the prize of himself.*

This is my thesis and to unfold its meaning and to show how biblical it is I think it will be helpful to take three snapshots from three different places: One from Romans 5, one from church history, and one from 1 Corinthians 15.

5.2 The Price and Prize of the Gospel in Romans 5

Keep in mind that the word "gospel" means good news, and in this case, it means God's good news for the world. What is the price and the prize of that good news according to Romans 5? Here's the price in Romans 5:6–8:

> *While we were still weak, at the right time Christ died for the ungodly. [7] For one will scarcely die for a righteous person—though perhaps for a good person one would dare even to die— [8] but God shows his love for us in that while we were still sinners, Christ died for us.*

The price of the gospel is the death of Christ. Verse 6: "Christ died for the ungodly." Verse 8: "Christ died for us." God loved us while we were sinners and paid a price so that we might have an infinite prize. That price was the death of his Son. And what was the prize that he bought for us when he paid that price? Verses 9-11:

> *Since, therefore, we have now been justified by his blood, much more shall we be saved by him from the wrath of God. [10] For if while we were enemies we were reconciled to God by the death of his Son, much more, now that we are reconciled, shall we be saved by his life. [11] More than that, we also rejoice in God through our Lord Jesus Christ, through whom we have now received reconciliation.*

What did God purchase for us by the price of his Son? Verse 9: "We have now been justified by his blood." And more. Verse 9b: Because of that justification we will be saved by him from wrath. What do we need to be saved from? The wrath of God. "Much more shall we be saved from the wrath of God" (verse 9). But is that the highest, best, fullest, most satisfying prize of the gospel?

Note that verse 11 begins with another "much more." Verse 10 ends: "We shall be saved by his life." And verse 11 takes it up a level: "More than that: we rejoice in God." That is the final and highest good of the good news. There is not another "much more" after that. There is only Paul's saying again how we got there. Verse 11b: "through our Lord Jesus Christ, through whom we have now received reconciliation."

The end of the gospel is "we rejoice in God." The highest, fullest, deepest, sweetest good of the gospel is God himself, enjoyed by his redeemed people. Hence the thesis: "God in Christ is the price and the prize of the gospel." God in Christ became the price (Romans 5:6–8), and God in Christ became the prize (Romans 5:11). The gospel is the good news that God bought for us the everlasting enjoyment of God. That's what I mean when I say "God is the gospel."

5.3 A Testimony from Church History

For five hundred years protestant Christians have summed up the gospel in terms of the five "solas," which is Latin for "only" or "alone." And all I do in giving you this summary is add one that is implicit in the others. So in these historical forms I would define the gospel like this:

As revealed with final authority in Scripture alone
the Gospel is the good news that
by faith alone
through grace alone
on the basis of Christ alone
for the glory of God alone
sinners have full and final joy in God alone.

All these affirmations are grounded in the Bible.

- *Scripture alone* is the final authority for revealing and defining the gospel of Christ (Galatians 1:9): "If anyone is preaching to you a gospel contrary to the one you received, let him be accursed." The apostolic delivery of the gospel is final and decisive.
- By *faith alone* (Romans 3:28): "We hold that one is justified by faith apart from works of the law." Faith plus nothing is the way we receive the gift of justification.
- Through *grace alone* (Ephesians 2:5, 8–9): "When we were dead in our trespasses, God made us alive together with Christ—by *grace* you have been saved—... For by *grace* you have been saved through faith. And this is not your own doing; it is the gift of God, not a result of works, so that no one may boast."
- On the basis of *Christ alone* (Hebrews 7:27): "Christ has no need, like those high priests, to offer sacrifices daily, first for his own sins and then for those of the people, since he did this once for all when he offered up himself." (See Hebrews 9:12; 10:10.) *Once for all* and decisively. Nothing can be added to the work of Christ

to cover our sins and that work cannot be repeated.

- For *the glory of God alone* (Ephesians 1:6): "God predestined us for adoption as sons through Jesus Christ… to the praise of the glory of his grace." God saved us in such a way that there would be no human boasting (Ephesians 2:9; 1 Corinthians 1:26–31), but all would show his glory.
- "Full and final joy in *God alone*" (Psalm 16:11; 73:25f): "In your presence there is fullness of joy; at your right hand are pleasures forevermore." "Whom have I in heaven but you? And there is nothing on earth that I desire besides you. My flesh and my heart may fail, but God is the strength of my heart and my portion forever."

This is the gospel as millions of Christians have thought about it for centuries, and we are happy to link arms with this great Reformation heritage: God in Christ *is* the price and the prize of the gospel.

5.4 The Price and Prize of the Gospel in 1 Corinthians 15

There are six important elements in 1 Corinthians 15, five of which are explicit in the text and one of which is implicit. Verses 1–4:

> *Now I would remind you, brothers, of the gospel I preached to you, which you received, in which you stand,* [2] *and by which you are being saved, if you hold fast to the word I preached to you—unless you believed in vain.* [3] *For I delivered to you as of first*

importance what I also received: that Christ died for our sins in accordance with the Scriptures,[4] *that he was buried, that he was raised on the third day in accordance with the Scriptures.*

Six Indispensable Elements of the Gospel

Here we see six elements of the gospel. If any of these six were missing, there would be no gospel.

1. The gospel is a *divine plan.* Verse 3b: "Christ died for our sins *in accordance with the Scriptures.*" In accordance with the Scriptures written hundreds of years before he died. Which means the gospel was planned by God long before it took place.

2. The gospel is a *historical event.* Verse 3b: "Christ died." The gospel is not mythology. It is not mere ideas or feelings. It is an event. And without the event there is no gospel.

3. The gospel is the *divine achievements* through that event—that death. Things God accomplished in the death of Jesus long before we ever existed. Verse 3b: "Christ died *for our sins.*" For our sins means this death had design in it. It was meant to accomplish something. It accomplished the covering of our sins (Colossians 2:14), the removal of God's wrath (Romans 8:3; Galatians 3:13), the purchase of eternal life (John 3:16). These are objective achievements of the work of Christ before they are applied to anyone.

4. The gospel is a *free offer of Christ for faith.* Verses 1–2:

"... the gospel I preached to you, which you received, in which you stand, 2 and by which you are being saved, if you hold fast to the word I preached to you—unless you *believed* in vain." The good news of God's achievements in Christ become ours by faith, by believing, by receiving. Not by giving a performance or by deserving or working. What God has done is free to all who will have it. It is received by faith. Without the free offer of Christ for faith there would be no gospel.

5. The gospel is an *application to believers* of what God achieved in the death of Jesus. So when we believe we are forgiven for our sins (Acts 10:43); we are justified (Romans 5:1); we receive eternal life (John 3:16) and dozens of other benefits (which is why I wrote a book called *Fifty Reasons Why Jesus Came to Die*). The gospel is the powerful personal application to us of what God achieved for us on the cross.

6. The gospel is the *enjoyment of fellowship with God himself.* This is implicit in the word "gospel," good news. If you ask: "What is the highest, deepest, most satisfying, all-encompassing good of the good news?" The answer is: God himself known and enjoyed by his redeemed people. This is made explicit in 1 Peter 3:18: "Christ suffered once for sins, the righteous for the unrighteous, *that he might bring us to God.*" All the other gifts of the gospel exist to make this one possible. We are forgiven so that our guilt does not keep us away from God. We are justified so that our condemnation does not keep us away from God. We are given eternal life now, with new bodies in the resurrection, so that we

> have the capacities for enjoying God to the fullest. Test your heart. Why do you want forgiveness? Why do you want to be justified? Why do you want eternal life? Is the decisive answer: "because I want to enjoy God?"

In summary then, "God in Christ is The Price and the Prize of the Gospel." The prize of the gospel is the Person who paid the price. The gospel-love God gives is ultimately the gift of himself. This is what we were made for. This is what we lost in our sin. This is what Christ came to restore. "In your presence there is fullness of joy; at your right hand are pleasures forevermore" (Psalm 16:11).

5.5 The Love of God Is the Gift of Himself

I offer the below quote to you on behalf of Christ. Indeed I urge you to receive it. It's free. All it takes is for you to see the beauty of Christ and receive him as your Treasure and your Lord and your Savior. This is what it means to believe the gospel. To give you one final enticement I will read the most beautiful description I have ever read of what I mean by saying God is the gospel and that the love of God is the gift of himself. It comes from Jonathan Edwards in 1731 when he was 28:

> *The redeemed have all their objective good in God. God himself is the great good which they are brought to the possession and enjoyment of by redemption. He is the highest good, and the sum of all that good which Christ purchased.*
>
> *God is the inheritance of the saints; he is the portion of their souls. God is their wealth and treasure, their*

food, their life, their dwelling place, their ornament and diadem, and their everlasting honor and glory. They have none in heaven but God; he is the great good which the redeemed are received to at death, and which they are to rise to at the end of the world. The Lord God, he is the light of the heavenly Jerusalem; and is the "river of the water of life" that runs, and the tree of life that grows, "in the midst of the paradise of God."

The glorious excellencies and beauty of God will be what will forever entertain the minds of the saints, and the love of God will be their everlasting feast. The redeemed will indeed enjoy other things; they will enjoy the angels, and will enjoy one another: but that which they shall enjoy in the angels, or each other, or in anything else whatsoever, that will yield them delight and happiness, will be what will be seen of God in them.[1]

Amen.

E. MORE ABOUT THE GOSPEL

How Is the Gospel the Power of God unto Salvation?

Let's dwell on the words of Romans 1:16: "for it [the gospel] is the power of God for salvation to everyone who believes."

I will take up only one question: What is this salvation that the gospel so powerfully brings about? By answering this question we will see how our faith relates to the gospel in bringing about our salvation.

"The gospel is the power of God for [unto] salvation."

Does this mean, "The gospel is the power of God to win converts"? I do think that is true, but I don't think that is what this statement in Romans 1:16 means. The reason I think it is true that the gospel converts people—brings them to faith and repentance—is because Romans 10:17 says, "So faith *comes* from hearing, and hearing by the word of Christ." And 1 Peter 1:23–25 says, "You have been born again not of seed which is perishable but imperishable, through the living and enduring word of God....and this is the word which was preached to you." So it is true that we are born of God and converted by means of hearing the powerful word of God, the gospel.

And it's true that this conversion is called "salvation" in the New Testament. For example, Ephesians 2:8–9: "For by grace you have been *saved* through faith; and that not of yourselves, it is the gift of God; not as a result of works, so that no one may boast." So conversion to Christ by faith is called "being saved." If you are a believer in Christ, you "have been saved." The Book of Romans should be precious beyond words to you, because, like no other book in the Bible, it unfolds for you what has already happened in God's saving you—your election, your predestination, your calling, your justification, your sanctification, and the obedience of faith. These are all part of the salvation that is already true of you through faith.

But what is the salvation that Paul has in mind in Romans 1:16? What does he mean when he says, "For [the gospel] is the power of God for salvation to everyone who believes"?

I think he has in mind not primarily the first event of conversion, but primarily *the final triumph of the gospel in bringing believers to eternal safety and joy in the presence of a holy and glorious God.*

There are four reasons why I think this is what he means. Looking at these reasons is the best way to unpack the meaning of the verse.

1. The power of the gospel is what frees us from being ashamed of the gospel.

"I am not ashamed of the gospel, for it is the power of God for salvation." But if this meant only that the gospel has the power to make converts, why would that solve the shame problem? Lots of religions make converts. Lots of different religious and secular movements win people over to their faith. When Paul said that the gospel has such a powerful effect that you don't have to be ashamed of it, did he simply mean that it does what other religions do? Is it that the gospel simply win converts? I don't think so.

Jesus triumphed over shame by looking at the future joy that was set before him as he died. I think this is what Paul, as well, has in mind in Romans 1:16. You don't have to be ashamed of the gospel because it doesn't just make converts; *it saves those converts utterly.* It brings them to final safety and ever-increasing joy in the presence of a glorious and holy God forever and ever. This is what makes us bold with the gospel—not that it can make converts (any religion can do that)—but that it is the only truth in the world that can really save people forever and bring them to everlasting joy with God.

2. "Salvation" is future-oriented elsewhere in Paul and the New Testament.

The second reason I think "salvation" in verse 16 refers to *the final triumph of the gospel in bringing believers to eternal safety and joy in the presence of a holy and glorious God* is that the phrase "for salvation" or "unto salvation" has this future-oriented meaning elsewhere in Paul and other New Testament writers.

For example, in 2 Thessalonians 2:13 Paul says, "God has chosen you from the beginning *for salvation* through sanctification by the Spirit and faith in the truth." Now here, salvation is not just what happens at conversion, which leads to sanctification, but salvation is what comes later "*through* sanctification," and is in the future. In other words, salvation is the future triumph that brings the saint into God's presence with everlasting joy.

Or again, in 2 Corinthians 7:10, Paul speaks to Christians who are already converted and saved, but need fresh repentance for their sins: "The sorrow that is according to the will of God produces a repentance without regret, *unto salvation*, but the sorrow of the world produces death." Here again "unto salvation" refers not to conversion, but to the final, future state of safety and joy in the presence of God. (See also 2 Timothy 3:15.)

Similarly, Hebrews 9:28 says, "Christ ... will appear a second time *for salvation* ... to those who eagerly await him." This final, complete salvation happens at the Second

Coming. 1 Peter 1:5 says, "[Believers] are protected by the power of God through faith *for salvation* ready to be revealed in the last time." This salvation is "ready to be revealed in the last time." It is not conversion. It is the last great work of God to rescue us and bring us to safety and joy in his presence forever.

In Romans 5:9–10, Paul talks about this future salvation as rescue from the final wrath of God:

> *Since, therefore, we have now been justified by his blood, [that's the present reality of salvation!] much more shall* we be saved by him from the wrath of God. *For if while we were enemies we were reconciled to God by the death of his Son [here again is the present reality of salvation!], much more, now that we are reconciled,* shall we be saved by his life.

In other words, the full experience of salvation, in Paul's thinking, is still future. Romans 13:11: "Salvation is nearer to us than when we believed."

So when Paul says in Romans 1:16 that "[the gospel] is the power of God unto salvation," I take him to mean that the gospel is the only message in the world that powerfully can bring a person not just to conversion, but to everlasting safety and joy in the presence of a holy and glorious God.

3. Ongoing belief is the condition for this salvation.

The third reason I think "salvation" in Romans 1:16 is *the final triumph of the gospel in bringing believers to eternal safety and joy in the presence of a holy and glorious God* is that ongoing belief is the condition for this salvation.

Notice that verse 16 does not say, "The gospel ... is the power of God to bring about faith and salvation." It says, "The gospel is the power of God for [unto] salvation to everyone who is believing [present tense in Greek, signifying continuous action]."

In other words, Paul's point here is not that the power of the gospel creates faith, but that, for those who have faith, the gospel brings about salvation. So the point is not that the gospel is the power for conversion to faith; the point is that the gospel is the power to bring about future salvation *through* a life of faith.

The tense of the verb "believe" here is crucial. It signifies ongoing action, not just the first act of faith when you were converted: "The gospel ... is the power of God unto salvation to everyone who *is believing*"—those who go on believing. It's the same as 1 Corinthians 15:1–2 where Paul says, "I preached to you [the gospel], which also you received, in which also you stand, by which also you are being saved, *if you hold fast the word which I preached to you, unless you believed in vain.*" Faith that does not persevere is a vain and empty faith—what James calls "dead faith" (James 2:17, 26).

So the point of Romans 1:16 is that you don't have to be ashamed of the gospel, because it is the only truth in the world which, if you go on banking on it day after day, will triumph over every obstacle and bring you to eternal safety and joy in the presence of a holy and glorious God.

4. Paul says the gospel is for believers, not just unbelievers.

The last reason I think "salvation" in Romans 1:16 is *the final triumph of the gospel in bringing believers to eternal safety and joy in the presence of a holy and glorious God* is that the verse is given as the reason Paul wants to preach the gospel to believers (not just unbelievers).

We've seen this, but look again. In verse 15 Paul says, "I am eager to preach the gospel to you also who are in Rome." He is eager to preach the gospel to "you"—you believers—not just unbelievers. Then he gives the reason: "because I am not ashamed of it, because it is the power of God unto salvation to all such believers."

So I conclude that the reason Paul is not ashamed of the gospel is that it is the only truth in all the world that will not let you down when you give your life to it in faith. It will bring you all the way through temptation and persecution and death and judgment into eternal safety and ever-increasing joy in the presence of a holy and glorious God. All the other "gospels" in the world that win so many converts will fail you in the end. Only one saves from the final wrath of God and leads to fullness of joy in his presence and pleasures at his right hand forever. Therefore, there is no need to be ashamed of it, no matter what others say or do. And oh how eager we should be to speak this gospel to believer and unbeliever alike!

Do you feed your faith day by day with the promises of this triumphant gospel? Do you, as a believer, go to the gospel day by day and savor its power in verses like Romans 8:32, "He who did not spare his own Son, but delivered him over for us all, how will he not also with him freely give us all things?" The gospel is the good news that God gave us his son, so as to obtain for us everything that would be good for us. Therefore the gospel is the power that gives us victory over temptation to despair and to pride and to greed and to lust. The gospel alone can triumph over every obstacle and bring us to eternal joy. Whatever it costs, stand in it, hold it fast, believe on it, feed on it, savor it, count it more precious than silver or gold. The gospel will save you. And it alone.

I love to tell the story; for those who know it best
seem hungering and thirsting to hear it, like the rest.
And when, in scenes of glory, I sing the new, new song,
'twill be the old, old story that I have loved so long.
I love to tell the story,
'twill be my theme in glory
To tell the old, old story
Of Jesus and his love.[2]

6. THE CALL TO GLOBAL MISSIONS

In 1890, Bethlehem Baptist Church (a 29-year-old Swedish Baptist Church at that time) sent members Mini and Ola Hanson to an unreached people group in Burma called the Kachin. They were known as vengeful, cruel, and treacherous. The King of Burma declared to Hanson when he got there, "So you are to teach the Kachins! Do you see my dogs over there? I tell you, it will be easier to convert and teach these dogs. You are wasting your life."

The Kachin were completely illiterate with no written language. Over the next 30 years Hanson collected 25,000 words and published a Kachin-English dictionary. In 1911 Hanson finished translating the New Testament. On August 11, 1926 he completed the Old Testament.

In a letter on August 14 of that year Hanson wrote: "It is with heartfelt gratitude that I lay this work at the feet of my Master. I'm conscious of the intelligible to all. Pray with us, that our divine Master may bless this work to the salvation of the whole Kachin race." Today virtually all Kachin can read and write in their own language, as well as Burmese, the national language. And there are over half a million Kachin Christians.[3]

So the legacy of missions at Bethlehem goes back over a hundred years. And it has been one of the highest privileges of my life, without any exaggeration, to be a part of sustaining and growing this legacy. I have often thought: *O Lord, if we falter as a church, if we stumble, if we drop the ropes, so many missionaries will fall.* Maintaining the strength of this church is not just about the saints here or the impact that we have on the Twin Cities. It's about the hundreds of global partners who have gone down in the mines on ropes held by this church.

6.1 A Powerful Image of the Missions Effort

Holding the rope has been a powerful image for us over the years. It comes from William Carey who blazed the trail to India in 1792 and saw his mission as a miner penetrating into a deep mine, which had never been explored, with no one to guide. He said to Andrew Fuller and John Ryland and his other pastor friends: "I will go down, if you will hold the rope." And John Ryland reports: "He took an oath from each of us, at the mouth of the pit, to this effect—that 'while we lived, we should never let go of the rope.'"[4]

Now as I bequeath the leadership of the church—of the mission, there are 109 families and single people (192 adults, 170 children, 362 souls!) that have put the ropes of their support in our hands. That is amazing and frightening and wonderful. What a privilege! We are all goers or senders, or disobedient. There are those who drop into mines, those who hold the ropes, and those who think it's not their business. Rejoice that you are part of a church that doesn't just *support*, but *sends* from our own number, over a hundred families and singles to take the gospel to the peoples of the world.

6.2 Do You Have a Compulsion to Go?

On an annual basis, Bethlehem's weekly focus on global missions has been a flashpoint in the missionary fires that burn all year long. Every year I conclude with a message where I invite a group of listeners to come to the front of the auditorium. I invite them to come in order to bear open witness to the wonderful work of God in their sense of calling to long-term, cross-cultural missions, and to seek clarity and confirmation and courage for that calling as we pray for them.

And the question is: "Has God been working in you—for twenty years, or twenty days or twenty minutes—to give you a compelling sense that, unless he shows you otherwise, you are moving, with his help, toward the nations longer term? (We love short-term missions, but that's not what this is about.) Has God been working in you a desire to go for at least two years and possibly more, crossing a culture to spread the best news in all the world—that Jesus Christ, the Son of God, came into the world to save sinners by dying in our place and rising again?

So what I am going to do, as part of our series on the thirty-year theological trademarks of Bethlehem, is give you ten biblical convictions that drive our commitment to global outreach—to world missions—at Bethlehem. And as I give you these I pray that they will burn in your soul—for some of you as a God-given compulsion to go, and for others as a God-given compulsion to send.

6.3 Ten Biblical Convictions on Global Missions

1. God is passionately committed to the fame of his name and that he be worshipped by all the peoples of the world, and this is not egomania, it is love.

Missions, global outreach, is joining God in his passion to love the nations by offering himself to them for overflowing joy of their praise.

› "Declare his glory among the nations, his marvelous works among all the peoples!" (Psalm 96:3).

› "Make known his deeds among the peoples, proclaim that his name is exalted" (Isaiah 12:4).

› God sends Jesus on his mission "in order that the Gentiles might glorify God for his mercy" (Romans 15:9).

› He does his mighty works in history "that [his] name might be proclaimed in all the earth" (Romans 9:17).

2. Therefore worship is the goal and the fuel of missions: Missions exists because worship doesn't.

Missions is our way of saying: *the joy of knowing Christ is not a private or tribal or national or ethnic privilege. It is for all.* And that's why we go. Because we have tasted the joy of worshiping Jesus, and we want all the families of the earth included. "All the ends of the earth shall remember and turn to the Lord, and all the families of the nations shall worship before you" (Psalm 22:27).

Seeking the worship of the nations is fueled by the joy of our own worship. You can't commend what you don't cherish. You can't proclaim what you don't prize. Worship is the fuel and the goal of missions.

3. People must be told about Jesus, because there is no salvation and no worship where the gospel of the crucified and risen Son of God is not heard and believed.

› "And there is salvation in no one else, for there is no other name under heaven given among men by which we must be saved" (Acts 4:12).

› "Faith comes from hearing, and hearing through the word of Christ" (Romans 10:17).

› "Whoever has the Son has life; whoever does not have the Son of God does not have life" (1 John 5:12).

› "Go therefore and make disciples of all nations" (Matthew 28:19).

There will be no salvation and no true worship among people who have not heard the gospel. Missions is essential for salvation.

4. God is committed to gathering worshipers from all the peoples of the world, not just all the countries of the world.

This is what "all nations" means in the great commission. Nations like Ojibwe, and Fulani and Kachin, not like the United States and Japan and Argentina. This is what Jesus bought with blood:

> *Worthy are you to take the scroll and to open its seals, for you were slain, and by your blood you ransomed people for God from every tribe and language and people and nation, and you have made them a kingdom and priests to our God, and they shall reign on the earth.* —Revelation 5:9–10

The gospel has already reached all the countries. But, according to the Joshua Project (www.joshuaproject.net) there are over 7,000 unreached peoples. That is why our mission statement says: "We exist to spread a passion for the supremacy of God in all things for the joy of all peoples [plural!] through Jesus Christ."

5. Therefore there is a critical need for Paul-type missionaries whose calling and passion is to take the gospel to peoples where there is no access to the gospel at all.

I am distinguishing Paul-type missionaries from Timothy-type missionaries. Timothy left his home and served cross culturally in a city (Ephesus) different from his own (Lystra). But Paul said in Romans 15:20, "I make it my ambition to preach the gospel, not where Christ has already been named." There is still much to do where Christ has been named. But oh how we need to pray for an army of hundreds of thousands with Paul's passion to reach the utterly unreached and unengaged peoples of the world.

6. We must send the global partners in a manner worthy of God.

This is why we have a missions staff and a missions budget and a missions nurture program and why we have Barnabas support teams for our missionaries. "You will do well to send them on their journey in a manner worthy of God" (3 John 1:6). This is why senders are crucial along with goers. We don't believe everyone is a frontier missionary. Frontier missionaries cross cultures and plant the church where it's not. But if we are not a goer, there is a great calling: Sender. And John says, Do it in a manner worthy of God.

7. It is fitting for us to have a wartime mindset in the use of our resources as long as peoples are without the gospel, and we have resources to send it.

In peace time the Queen Mary was a luxury liner but in the second world war she became a troop carrier. Instead of bunks three high they were stacked seven high. Instead of 18-piece place settings, there were rations with fork and knife. You allocate your resources differently if it's wartime. And it is wartime. The battles are more constant than any in our world wars, and the losses are eternal.

The Macedonians in 2 Corinthians 8:2 are a model for us in the face of great need: "In a severe test of affliction, their abundance of joy and their extreme poverty have overflowed in a wealth of generosity on their part." Oh that we would deepen in our grasp of the urgency of the hour and remember that ultimately we don't own anything. God owns us and all we have. And he cares about how it goes in the war effort to reach the nations with the gospel Jesus died to send.

8. Prayer is a war-time walkie-talkie, not a domestic intercom.

"I chose you and appointed you," Jesus said, "that you should go and bear fruit... *so that* whatever you ask the Father in my name, he may give it to you" (John 15:16). I give you a mission so that your prayers will be fruitful. Prayer is for mission. It is mainly for those on the front lines of the war effort to call in to headquarters to send help.

One of the reasons our prayer malfunctions is that we try to treat it like a domestic intercom for calling the butler for another pillow in the den rather than treating it like a wartime walkie-talkie for calling down the power of the Holy Spirit in the battle for souls.

9. Suffering is not only the price for being in missions, it is God's plan for getting the job done.

› "If they have called the master of the house Beelzebul, how much more will they malign those of his household." —Matthew 10:25

› "They will deliver you up to tribulation and put you to death, and you will be hated by all nations for my name's sake." —Matthew 24:9

› "Behold, I am sending you out as sheep in the midst of wolves." —Matthew 10:16

This is not just the price many must pay. This is God's

strategy for victory. His Son won the victory this way. So will we. "They have conquered him by the blood of the Lamb and by the word of their testimony, for they loved not their lives even unto death" (Revelation 12:11). They conquered (not were conquered) by testimony and death.

10. The global cause of Christ cannot fail. And nothing you do in this cause is in vain.

Jesus said, "All authority in heaven and on earth has been given to me. Therefore go, make disciples" (Matthew 28:18). Not some authority. All. He cannot be defeated. "I will build my church, and the gates of hell shall not prevail against it" (Matthew 16:18). "This gospel of the kingdom will be proclaimed throughout the whole world as a testimony to all nations, and then the end will come" (Matthew 24:14). He has ransomed a people for all the nations. And he will have them. "I have other sheep that are not of this fold. I must bring them also, and they will listen to my voice. So there will be one flock, one shepherd" (John 10:16).

There are more, but those are ten of our main biblical convictions that drive Bethlehem's commitment to global outreach. And for some of you, as you have been reading, these convictions have become, again, a confirmation that God is leading you into long-term, cross-cultural missions.

Amen.

F. MORE ABOUT MISSIONS

Four Motives for Missions from John 10:16

> *And I have other sheep that are not of this fold. I must bring them also, and they will listen to my voice. So there will be one flock, one shepherd.* —John 10:16

There are four things in John 10:16 that should fill us to overflowing with confidence in our missions dreaming and planning and labor.

1. Jesus has other sheep.

Christ has people besides those already converted—other people besides us. "I have other sheep that are not of this fold." There will always be people who argue that the doctrine of predestination makes missions unnecessary. But they are wrong. It does not make missions unnecessary; it makes missions hopeful.

John Alexander, a former president of Inter-Varsity, said in a message at Urbana '67, "At the beginning of my missionary career I said that if predestination were true, I could not be a missionary. Now after 20 years of struggling with the hardness of the human heart, I say I could never be a missionary unless I believed in the doctrine of predestination." It gives hope that Christ most certainly has a people among the nations. "I have other sheep."

It was precisely this truth that encouraged the apostle Paul when he was downcast in Corinth. Acts 18:9–10: "And the Lord said to Paul one night in a vision, 'Do not be afraid, but speak and do not be silent; for I am with you, and no man shall attack you to harm you; for I have many people in this city.'"

"I have other sheep that are not of this fold." It is a promise full of hope for those who dream about new fields of missionary labor.

2. These sheep are scattered outside the present fold.

The verse implies that the "other sheep" that Christ has are scattered outside the present fold. This is made explicit in John 11:51–52, where John explains a word of prophecy spoken by Caiaphas, the high priest, "He did not say this of his own accord, but being high priest that year he prophesied that Jesus should die for the nation, and not for the nation only, but to gather into one the children of God who are scattered abroad."

Evangelism for the apostle John is the ingathering of the children of God. Of course, in John 1:12–13 it says that we become children of God by being born again and receiving Christ. This doesn't have to be a contradiction. John 11:52 simply means that God has already predestined who will be delivered from the slavery to sin and unbelief and become children of God by faith; and so he calls these chosen ones "children of God" because from the divine perspective they are certainly going to be reached and saved.

But the point for our encouragement in missionary strategy is that they are *scattered*. They are not all pocketed in one or two places. They are scattered everywhere.

The way John put it when he wrote the Book of Revelation was this: "for you were slain, and by your blood you ransomed people for God from every tribe and language and people and nation."

The ransomed children of God will be found in every people reached by the gospel. And that is a great encouragement to get on with the task of frontier missions and to reach the hidden peoples.

3. The Lord is committed to his lost sheep.

The Lord has committed himself to bring his lost sheep home. He will do it. "I have other sheep that are not of this fold; I must bring them also." *He* will bring them.

This does not mean, as some of the hyper-Calvinists thought it did in Carey's day, that Christ will gather in his sheep without asking us! In John 17:18 and 20:21 Jesus says, "As the Father has sent me, even so send I you." We continue the mission of Christ. So Jesus prays in 17:20, "I do not pray for these [his disciples] only but also for those who believe in me through their word."

In other words, just as the voice of the shepherd called his sheep from Jesus' own lips in Palestine, so he still speaks today through the gospel and calls his sheep by name, and they hear his voice and follow him. He does it. But not without us!

This is the wonder of the gospel. When it is preached truthfully in the power of the Spirit, it is not merely the word of man. It is the word of God (1 Thessalonians 2:13).

In other words, even today in the gospel it is just as true as it was in Jesus's day, "My sheep hear *my* voice, and I know them, and they follow me" (John 10:27). It is Christ who calls in the gospel. Christ gathers. We are only witnesses. That is why Paul said in Romans 15:18, "I will not venture to speak of anything except what Christ has wrought through me to win obedience from the Gentiles."

So we can take heart: all authority in heaven and on earth has been given to the Son of God and he declares, "I must bring in my other sheep." He will do it.

4. The sheep will come

This implies the final word of hope from John 10:16: *if he brings them, they will come*! "I have other sheep that are not of this fold; I must bring them also, and *they will listen to my voice*." None of Christ's sheep finally reject his word. What else can keep you going in a hard and unresponsive place of ministry, except that God reigns and those whom the Father has chosen will heed the voice of the Son?

Consider the story of Peter Cameron Scott who was born in 1867 and founded the African Inland Mission. He had tried twice to serve in Africa but had to come home both times with malaria. The third attempt was especially joyful because he was joined by his brother John. But the joy evaporated as John fell victim to the fever. Scott buried his brother all by himself, and at the grave rededicated himself to preach the gospel. But again his health broke and he had to return to England utterly discouraged.

But in London something wonderful happened. We read about it in Ruth Tucker's *From Jerusalem to Irian Jaya*—a book that I hope all of you will read. He needed a fresh source of inspiration and he found it at a tomb in

Westminster Abbey that held the remains of a man who had inspired so many others in their missionary service to Africa. The spirit of David Livingstone seemed to be prodding Scott onward as he knelt reverently and read the inscription,

> *Other sheep I have which are not of this fold; them also I must bring.*

Scott would return to Africa and lay down his life, if need be, for the cause for which this great man had lived and died.

> *Lord, put a thorn in our cushion and courage in our hearts. And send us with joy and confidence to the unreached peoples of the earth. Give us a passion to be your instruments for the ingathering of the elect through all the world. Amen.*

7. LIVING THE CHRISTIAN LIFE

We ought always to give thanks to God for you, brothers, as is right, because your faith is growing abundantly, and the love of every one of you for one another is increasing. [4] Therefore we ourselves boast about you in the churches of God for your steadfastness and faith in all your persecutions and in the afflictions that you are enduring. [5] This is evidence of the righteous judgment of God, that you may be considered worthy of the kingdom of God, for which you are also suffering—[6] since indeed God considers it just to repay with affliction those who afflict you, [7] and to grant relief to you who are afflicted as well as to us, when the Lord Jesus is revealed from heaven with his mighty angels [8] in flaming fire, inflicting vengeance on those who do not know God and on those who do not obey the gospel of our Lord Jesus. [9] They will suffer the punishment of eternal destruction, away from the presence of the Lord and from the glory of his might, [10] *when he comes on that day to be glorified in his saints, and to be marveled at among all who have believed, because our testimony to you was believed.* [11] *To this end we always pray for you, that our God may make you worthy of his calling and may fulfill every resolve for good and every work of faith by his power,* [12] *so that the name of our Lord Jesus may be glorified in you, and you in him, according to the grace of our God and the Lord Jesus Christ.* —2 Thessalonians 1:3–12

I preached on this text the last Sunday of 1985. Little did I know that I was uncovering in verses 11 and 12 the foundations of what would become one of our most practical and important thirty-year theological trademarks, namely, living by faith in future grace. So what I would like to do here is summarize these two verses and then flesh out what it means to live by faith in future grace and how faith in future grace becomes the conduit of God's power into your life.

7.1 Eight Crucial Things to See in 2 Thessalonians 1:1–12

There are eight absolutely crucial things to see in Paul's prayer.

1. The Calling of God

First, there is the *calling of God*. Verse 11: "That our God may make you worthy of his calling." This calling is our glorious destiny in God's kingdom and glory. That's what Paul says in 1 Thessalonians 2:12: "We charged you to walk in a manner worthy of God, who calls you into his own kingdom and glory." Your calling is to be in the kingdom of God and to share the glory of God, as we will see in just a moment.

2. Being Made Worthy

Second, there is our *being made worthy* of God's calling. Verse 11: "... that our God may make you worthy of his calling." Being made worthy doesn't mean being made deserving. It means being made suitable or fitting or appropriate because of the worth of another. So we would say, I need to fix up this room because the Queen of England is going to stay with us and the room needs to be worthy of her dignity. It needs to be fitting, suitable, appropriate. She didn't decide to come because the room is beautiful. The room should be made beautiful because she's coming. So we are being made suitable for our calling into God's kingdom and glory.

3. Fulfillment of Good Resolves

Third, there is the *fulfillment of good resolves.* Verse 11: "That our God may make you worthy of his calling and *may fulfill every resolve for good.*" The Christian life is a resolving, planning, purposing, intending life. We have minds and wills and God expects that we will use them to form resolves and plans and purposes, according to his will. These resolves are to be fulfilled. But how?

4. Fulfilled by God's Power

That's the fourth thing: *by the power of God*. Verse 11: "That our God may make you worthy of his calling and may fulfill every resolve for good and every work of faith *by his power*." If our resolves were fulfilled by our power we would get the glory. But it will be plain in just a moment, that God intends to get the glory for the fulfillment of our good resolves. So he fulfills them by *his* power, not ours. So our duty is to tap into his power. *How*?

5. Living by Faith

That's the fifth thing: *by faith*. Verse 11: "That our God may make you worthy of his calling and may fulfill every resolve for good and every *work of faith* by his power." When God fulfills a resolve for good, it becomes a work of faith because the means by which we receive the power to fulfill the resolve and turn it into a deed is faith. So the deed or the work or the act is called a "work of faith" or a "deed of faith" or an "act of faith." So from God's side the resolve became a deed by God's power. And from our side the resolve became a deed by faith—faith in that power. By faith we trusted God for the power to fulfill the resolve and, by that power, through that faith, the resolve became a deed or work, a work of faith. This sin was defeated. The righteousness was performed, because we looked away from ourselves to God and all his powerful effects in our lives.

6. Jesus Is Glorified

The sixth thing to see in this text is that *the name of Jesus is glorified* when God's power fulfills our resolves and through faith turns them into deeds. Verse 12: "... so that the name of our Lord Jesus may be glorified in you." That is, God fulfills our resolves by his power through our faith so that the name of Jesus gets glory. This assumes that the power of God is coming to us because of Jesus. Because Jesus has died for us, God's power is now not against us but for us. So when that power enables us to turn our resolves into deeds of love, Jesus and the Father get the glory.

7. We Are Glorified in Him

Seventh, not only is Jesus glorified in us, but *we are glorified in him*. Verse 12: "... so that the name of our Lord Jesus may be glorified in you, *and you in him*." In other words, as Jesus glorifies himself in purchasing the power of God to be made worthy of our calling, we too are being glorified. And the day will come when that slow process in this world will be completed in the twinkling of an eye, and we will "be saved to sin no more." This is the calling for which we are being made worthy, suitable.

8. It Is All of Grace

Finally, eighth, all of this process of being made worthy of our calling and fulfilling our good resolves and doing good works by faith in God's power, is "according to the grace of our God and the Lord Jesus Christ." Verse 12: "... so that the name of our Lord Jesus may be glorified in you, and you in him, *according to the grace of our God and the Lord Jesus Christ*." It was all of grace. The power of God that comes to us moment by moment fulfilling our resolves in works of faith is the power of grace.

Now let me put the eight pieces together in the order

that they actually work. Paul ended with the foundation of everything—*the grace of God and the Lord Jesus Christ*. Let's start with the foundation and build the structure of the Christian life with these eight pieces. If you are a Christian this is your life.

Everything starts with and is built on the grace of God. That grace is expressed in *God's power* toward his children. See the end of verse 11: "by his power." That gracious power which God exerts toward his children is appropriated, received, tapped into *by faith*. The way we experience the power of God is by trusting him to be for us everything we need so that good resolves become deeds of faith.

The effect of this power, as we trust him for it, is to fulfill our resolves for good and turn them into acts, deeds, which he calls *works of faith*. Thus the life of the Christian is lived by faith. Christianity is not a will-power religion. We will things. We resolve. We plan. We form purposes. But as we engage our wills to act we look to God. And we treasure him. We love him. We trust him that the power will be given to fulfill the resolve.

7.2 A Panorama of the Christian Life

In this way, then, we are made worthy of our calling. A life of God-dependent obedience is a life fitting, or appropriate, or suitable for our calling into God's kingdom and glory. And this being made worthy is the first stage in our being fully glorified in Christ and Christ's being fully glorified through us.

So when you stand back and look at these two verses they are an amazing panorama of the Christian life and of the meaning of existence. Everything flows from the free grace of God in Christ. And everything is moving toward the fullest glory of God in us and through us. And between the foundation of grace and the goal of glory there is the power of grace daily arriving in our lives through faith turning daily resolves and plans and purposes into deeds of faith, and fitting us for glory. Live these verses!

That's your life as a Christian. Daily, hourly, tapping into the flow of God's grace for the awakening and fulfilling of your good resolves, so that as you are made increasingly worthy of his calling—fitted for his kingdom and glory—Jesus gets more and more glory in your life.

7.3 What It Means for the Everyday

Now let me step back and draw out of these two verses—this amazing picture of the Christian life—what I mean by the thirty-year theological trademark of living by faith in future grace. Because what I mean is all right here either explicitly or implicitly.

Grace, in the New Testament, as we have seen, is not only God's disposition to do good for us when we don't deserve it—undeserved favor. It is also a power from God that acts in our lives and makes good things happen in us and for us. Paul said that we fulfill our resolves for good "by his power" (verse 11). And then he adds at the end of verse 12, "according to the grace of our God and the Lord Jesus Christ." That power that actually works in our lives to make Christ-exalting obedience possible is an extension of the grace of God.

You can see this also in 1 Corinthians 15:10: "By the *grace* of God I am what I am, and his *grace* toward me was not in vain. On the contrary, I worked harder than any of them, though it was not I, but the *grace* of God that is with me." So grace is an active, present, transformative, obedience-enabling power.

Therefore this grace, which moves in power from God to you at a point in time, is both past and future. It has already done something for you or in you and therefore is past. And it is about to do something in you and for you, and so it is future—both five seconds away and five million years away.

God's grace is ever cascading over the waterfall of the present from the inexhaustible river of grace coming to us from the future into the ever-increasing reservoir of grace in the past. In the next five minutes, you will receive sustaining grace flowing to you from the future, and you will accumulate another five minute's worth of grace in the reservoir of the past.

7.4 Why We Should Be Grateful

The proper response to grace that you have experienced in the past is gratitude—a profoundly humble and transforming spirit in itself. And the proper response to grace promised to you in the future is faith. We are thankful for past grace, and we are confident in future grace. This is where I get the idea of faith in future grace. That's what Paul is talking about in 2 Thessalonians 2:11–12. We fulfill our good resolves by the power of grace arriving second by second as we trust God for it on the basis of Christ's work. And so we live in those moments by faith in the constant arrival of future grace.

It is not wrong to say that we trust in past grace—like the grace God showed us at the cross and in our new birth—but what we mean by that is: *We believe that because of these acts of past grace—the cross and the new birth—a river of future grace will never, ever stop flowing to us for all eternity.*

I just read this week in my devotions: "Christ is able to save to the uttermost those who draw near to God through him, since he always lives to make intercession for them" (Hebrews 7:25). Christ died for us and he lives for us. And because his death is all-purchasing, and his life is all-providing, grace will never stop flowing to us. Therefore to trust in past grace means to draw from it confidence in future grace.

So even though our faith is founded on decisive acts of past redeeming grace, the way faith works moment by moment to turn our resolves for good into deeds of purity and love (patience, kindness, meekness, goodness, faithfulness, self-control) is by looking up and forward to the boundless fountain of grace that comes to us through a river of promises for every moment of the day. We live by faith in the ever-arriving power of future grace.

7.5 Faith in Jesus Means Being Satisfied in Him

Here's another aspect of this thirty-year theological trademark. When we speak of faith—faith in future grace—we mean being satisfied with all that God promises to be for us in Christ. Jesus said, "Whoever believes in me shall never thirst" (John 6:35). In other words: *believing in me means receiving me as the satisfier of the thirst of your soul.* Being satisfied with all that God promises to be for us in Christ.

Faith is not only a serious assent to the truth of God's promises, it is also a satisfying embrace of Christ in those promises. When Paul says, "I count everything as loss because of the surpassing worth of knowing Christ" (Philippians 3:8), he means that moment by moment in every situation Christ satisfies. "I have learned in whatever situation I am," Paul said, "to be content. I know how to be brought low, and I know how to abound. In any and every circumstance, I have learned the secret of facing plenty and hunger, abundance and need. I can do all things through him who strengthens me" (Philippians 4:11–13).

Paul is "content"—satisfied—in every circumstance. How? Because he has learned a secret. What? "I have learned to trust him for moment by moment strengthening." "I can do all things through him who strengthens me." The future grace of all that God is for me in Christ, arriving every moment of my life, in every circumstance, for every need, is enough. It satisfies. I am content. That is what we mean by faith in future grace.

So when Paul says in 2 Thessalonians 1:11 that God fulfills our good resolves by his power through our faith according to his grace, he means that we defeat sin and we do righteousness by faith in future grace, that is, by being satisfied with all that God promises to be for us in Christ in the next five minutes, five weeks, five months, five years, five decades, and five centuries, and five million ages of ages.

7.6 Six Examples of God's Promises in Your Life

1. If you set your heart to give sacrificially and generously, the power of God to fulfill this resolve will come to you as you trust his future grace in the promise: "My God will supply every need of yours according to his riches in glory in Christ Jesus" (Philippians 4:19). And the promise: "Whoever sows bountifully will also reap bountifully" (2 Corinthians 9:6). And the promise: "God is able to make all grace abound to you, so that having all sufficiency in all things at all times, you may abound in every good work" (2 Corinthians 9:8).

2. If you set your heart to return good for evil, the power of God to fulfill this resolve will come to you as you trust his future grace in the promise: "Blessed are you when others revile you and persecute you and utter all kinds of evil against you falsely on my account. Rejoice and be glad, for your reward is great in heaven" (Matthew 5:11–12).

3. If you set your heart to renounce pornography, the power of God to fulfill this resolve will come to you as you trust his future grace in the promise: "Blessed are the pure in heart, for they shall see God" (Matthew 5:8). "It is better that you tear out your eye than that your whole body be thrown into hell" (Matthew 5:29). Much better. Wonderfully better. All-satisfyingly better.

4. If you set your heart to speak out for Christ when the opportunity comes, the power of God to fulfill this resolve will come to you as you trust his future grace in

the promise: "Do not be anxious how you are to speak or what you are to say, for what you are to say will be given to you in that hour" (Matthew 10:19).

5. If you set your heart to risk your life by ministering to the needy in a dangerous place, the power of God to fulfill this resolve will come to you as you trust his future grace in the promise: "To live is Christ, and to die is gain" (Philippians 1:21). "Don't fear those who kill the body but cannot kill the soul... Are not two sparrows sold for a penny? And not one of them will fall to the ground apart from your Father. But even the hairs of your head are all numbered" (Matthew 10:28–30).
6. If you set your heart to invite some for dinner who cannot repay you, the power of God to fulfill this resolve will come to you as you trust his future grace in the promise: "You will be blessed, because they cannot repay you. For you will be repaid at the resurrection of the just" (Luke 14:13–14).

May God increase our daily faith in his inexhaustible, blood-bought, Christ-exalting future grace!

G. MORE ABOUT THE CHRISTIAN LIFE

Build Your Life on the Mercies of God

> *I appeal to you therefore, brothers, by the mercies of God, to present your bodies as a living sacrifice, holy and acceptable to God, which is your spiritual worship.* —Romans 12:1

"I appeal to you therefore, brothers, *by the mercies of God...*"

Just think of this: Of all the things that Paul could have picked out from Romans 1–11 as the root and foundation of your new life in Christ, he picks out *the mercies of God.* What an amazing statement! Having written of God's wrath and righteousness and judgment, and of our fall and sin and death, and of Christ's death and resurrection, and of justification by faith alone, and of the coming of the Spirit to sanctify us and keep us, and of God's absolute sovereignty in his faithfulness to the elect and to Israel—having said all of that, he picks out this one great reality as the sum, or the height, of it all, and says, therefore, by *the mercies of God* I appeal to you.

This is not careless. Look at Romans 15:8–9: "For I tell you that Christ became a servant to the circumcised to show God's truthfulness, *in order to confirm the promises given to the patriarchs, and in order that the Gentiles might glorify God for his mercy.*" There it is. The aim of all 11 chapters—all 16 chapters—is that we might make the mercy of God look great among the nations.

O Christian, let's build our lives on the mercies of God. Let's say, "Because of the mercies of God in Christ I will live the life of Romans 12–16." You know we are on the right track here when you just walk down through chapter 12 and look at all the mercy that is going to flow out of us when we build our lives on the mercy of God.

- Verse 8 (near the end): "the one who does acts of mercy, [let him do it] with cheerfulness."
- Verse 9: "Let love be genuine."

- Verse 13: "Contribute to the needs of the saints."
- Verse 14: "Bless those who persecute you."
- Verse 15b: "Weep with those who weep."
- Verse 16b: "Associate with the lowly."
- Verse 17: "Repay no one evil for evil."
- Verse 19: "Never avenge yourselves."
- Verse 20: "If your enemy is hungry, feed him; if he is thirsty, give him something to drink."

We are entering a world of mercy, as we move into Romans 12–16. Why? Because our lives are built on something. Rooted in something. They are built on the mercies of God. Our lives are rooted in the mercies of God. Our lives are founded on the mercies of God.

The word mercy here implies not only forgiveness for the guilty, but especially tenderhearted compassion for the helpless and desperate. This is what we expect after Romans 1–11. Look for it in Romans 5:6–8:

> *For while we were still weak, at the right time Christ died for the ungodly. For one will scarcely die for a righteous person—though perhaps for a good person one would dare even to die—but God shows his love for us in that while we were still sinners, Christ died for us.*

Did you hear both sides of mercy? We were weak and helpless (that's one side), and we were sinners and guilty (that's the other side). Mercy responds to both. Mercy *forgives* the guilty and mercy *pities* the helpless.

Have you built your life on that? Or maybe I should ask, Have you saturated your life with that? Have the mercies of God in saving you sunk to the center and core of your life, so that you are living from a deep spring of humble, brokenhearted happiness in the God of mercy?

Would you pray for me to be this way? This is what I long for. At the core of my being—where my unpremeditated words and facial expressions and grunts and twitches come from—at the core of my being to be swimming, childlike, in the forgiving, compassionate mercy of God. I will pray this for you too.

How else will we love our enemies at home and on the mission field and return good for evil, when we are slandered because of our stand on the inerrancy and authority of the Bible, or on the meaning of marriage, or on racial justice, or the horror of partial-birth abortion, or the message that there is no way of salvation except through Jesus Christ? If our lives are not built on and saturated by the mercies of God in Christ, how will we stay merciful and magnify the Lord?

And you know, don't you, that mercy is not spineless. Look at the first two phrases of Romans 12:9: "Let love be genuine. *Abhor* what is evil."

"Abhor" is a really strong word. When you love deeply, you must hate passionately what destroys the beloved. But mercy weeps while it hates. Mercy hates evil, but in our personal relationships repays no one evil for evil (verse 17). Mercy knows what it's like to be hurt and offended, but does not avenge itself (verse 19). Mercy knows what it's like to have enemies, but says, "If your enemy is hungry, feed him."

Mercy is not weak. It has an unbreakable backbone, but is very soft to the touch.

May God encourage you and enable you by his Spirit to build your life on the mercies of God revealed in Jesus Christ. Receive these mercies. Entrust your life to them. Embrace them for the forgiveness of your sins and all the help you need to live a life of mercy.

The Life That Overcomes by Faith

How do we get to the point in our lives where the commandments of God are not a burden but a joy?

1 John 5:4–5 gives the answer. The commandments are not burdensome "because whatever is born of God overcomes the world; and this is the victory that overcomes the world, our faith. Who is it that overcomes the world but he who believes that Jesus is the Son of God?"

Verse 4 says that two things overcome the world: 1) that which is born of God, and 2) our faith.

Recall the relationship between faith and new birth in 1 John 5:1: every one who has faith has been born of God. New birth gives rise to faith in the promises of Christ. And this faith overcomes the world. And that takes away the burdensomeness of the commandments of God.

How does this work? What is the connection between the burdensomeness of the commandments of God and the world? It seems to be twofold: the commandments of God are burdensome to us on the one hand because the world tempts us to believe that obeying God's commandments is not as satisfying as disobeying them, and we tend to agree with the world, and on the other hand, there is something in us that loves to agree with the world. Before new birth we are "of the world" (4:5). Anything contrary to the lust of the flesh and the lust of the eyes and pride in possessions is a great burden and folly to unregenerate man.

It's a burden to be sexually chaste if you believe the message of the world that fornication or adultery really will give you more satisfaction. It's a burden to be honest on your tax returns if you believe the message of the world that more money would bring you satisfaction. It's a burden to witness to a colleague if you believe the message of the world that Christians are foolish and getting egg on your face is to be avoided at all costs. It's a burden to say, "I'm sorry; I was wrong," if you believe the message of the world that more satisfaction comes from keeping up the front of strength.

But if the world could be overcome, then the commandments of God would not be burdensome. They would be the way of joy and peace and satisfaction. What can overcome the temptations of the world? What can unmask the lies of the world?

Answer: God can. And he does it by causing us to be born again so that we can see the infinite superiority of the promises of Christ over the promises of the world. The result is that we trust Christ and by trusting him overcome the temptations of the world.

Faith says to every temptation of the world: "*No. Be gone*! I know where true satisfaction is to be found. God has loved me with an infinite love. He promises to work everything together for good for those who love him. He withholds no good thing from those who walk uprightly. Nothing you offer can compare to the joy of his fellowship now and the glory to be revealed hereafter. World, you have lost your power. I have become the glad slave of a Good Master. His yoke is easy and the burden of his commandments is light."

The Lord holds out many good things to you here. If you want to know that your love for others is real and not just self-deception, if you want to have the power to obey the commandments of God, if you want to find a life that is loving and at the same time not burdensome, if you want to overcome the deceptive power of the world, then consider the infinite superiority of the Son of God and put your faith in his forgiveness for your sins and his promises for your future. Whoever has the Son has life!

8. THE PERSEVERANCE OF THE SAINTS

Take care, brothers, lest there be in any of you an evil, unbelieving heart, leading you to fall away from the living God. [13] *But exhort one another every day, as long as it is called "today," that none of you may be hardened by the deceitfulness of sin.* [14] *For we have come to share in Christ, if indeed we hold our original confidence firm to the end.* [15] *As it is said, "Today, if you hear his voice, do not harden your hearts as in the rebellion."* —Hebrews 3:12–15

8.1 Will You Endure in Faith?

Events of upheaval and turmoil around the world should serve as a warning to us that the day will come, sooner or later, when the hostility of man will not be containable by human force. It will burst the dam of restraint and flood to your very door. And the most urgent question for all the followers of Jesus Christ will be: "Will our faith in

Jesus endure? Or will we give way to fear and unbelief and anger and vengeance?"

The prophet Daniel describes a time when one of the rulers of the last days "will speak words against the Most High, and shall *wear out* the saints of the Most High" (Daniel 7:25). And in the Book of Revelation, the apostle John describes the time like this: "If anyone is to be taken captive, to captivity he goes; if anyone is to be slain with the sword, with the sword must he be slain. Here is a call for the *endurance* and faith of the saints" (Revelation 13:10).

The crucial question for you in these days—and those days—is "will you endure?" Will your faith bear up under the assaults that are coming? Or will you be "worn out" and give up the faith and join the unbelieving illusion of safety? This is the question of perseverance. The question of eternal security, the topic of this sermon.

The doctrine we are talking about today goes by different names and has an urgent and practical application to our life together. Some call it the doctrine of eternal security. Some call it the doctrine of perseverance. And the practical application is that, whichever you call it, the process is a community project. That is, you and I are essential in helping each other persevere to the end in faith, and not make shipwreck of our souls.

8.2 A Theological Overview on Perseverance

The signature text that we have returned to many times over these decades is Hebrews 3:12–15. So I think it would be helpful to sketch a three-point theology of perseverance on the basis of these four verses, and their implications for your life. And then, I will show the wider basis for this in Scripture, its relation to the cross of our Lord Jesus, and close with some practical applications to your life in families and small groups.

1. The call to endure is real.

Hebrews 3:12, "Take care, brothers, lest there be in any of you an evil, unbelieving heart, leading you to fall away from the living God." This is a clear call to all believers ("brothers") to persevere in faith. Not to give way to unbelief. Not to "wear out." It's a call to endure. To last. To keep the faith to the end. "Don't let your heart become evil, and unbelieving. Don't fall away from the living God." This is a real danger spoken to the church. Those who blow it off because your doctrine of eternal security won't allow it are in the most danger.

2. We each are a means for one another's endurance.

Hebrews 3:13, "But [in contrast to giving way to a heart of unbelief] exhort one another every day, as long as it is called 'today,' that none of you may be hardened by the deceitfulness of sin." Then in verse 15 he does what he tells us to do. He gives such an exhortation from Psalm 95:7, "Today, if you hear his voice, do not harden your hearts as in the rebellion."

So point #2 is that one of the essential means of not becoming hardened—the protection against an evil heart of unbelief—is the other believers around you speaking faith-sustaining words into your life. Your family, your friends, your small group. "Exhort one another every day." That is, speak words of faith-sustaining truth into each other's lives. Paul said in Ephesians 4:29, "Only let out of your mouth what is good for building up, as fits the occasion, that it may give grace to those who hear."

So the second point of this theology of perseverance is that God has designed his church so that its members endure to the end in faith *by means of* giving and receiving faith-sustaining words from each other. You and I are the instruments by which God preserves the faith of his children. Perseverance is a community project. Just like God is not going to evangelize the world without human, faith-awakening voices, neither is he going to preserve his church without human faith-sustaining voices. And clearly from the words, "exhort one another" (verse 13), it means all of us, not just preachers. We depend on each other to endure in faith to the end.

3. Persevering in faith is evidence that we are in Christ.

Verse 14: Exhort each other, and help each other hold onto your confidence, "For [because] we *have come* to share in Christ, if indeed we *hold* our original confidence firm to the end." This is one of the most important verses in the book of Hebrews, because it establishes that if a person *has come* to share in Christ, that person will most certainly persevere to the end in faith. Look at the logic and the verb tenses carefully. Everything hangs on this.

Verse 14: "We *have come* to share in Christ, if indeed we *hold* our original confidence firm to the end." Notice, he does not say, "if we hold our confidence to the end." Which means that enduring to the end doesn't get you a share in Christ. It proves you already had a share in Christ. Perseverance is the evidence of being born again in Christ, not the means to it.

Or to put the same point negatively: If you don't hold your confidence in Christ to the end, what would it show? It would show that you "*had not come* to share in Christ." So the negative of verse 14 would read, "We *have not come* to share in Christ, if indeed we *do not hold* our original confidence firm to the end."

So you see what this implies about eternal security? It says: if you have come to share in Christ—that is, if you are born again, if you are truly converted, if you are justified and forgiven through saving faith—you cannot fail to persevere. You *will* hold your confidence in Christ to the end.

The logic is identical with 1 John 2:19. "They went out from us, but they were not of us; for if they had been of us, they would have continued with us. But they went out, that it might become plain that they all are not of us" (1 John 2:19). "If they had been of us, they would have continued with us," is the same as "If you truly share in Christ, you will hold your confidence to the end."

So here's the summary of our three-point theology of perseverance.

1. Don't let your heart become evil and unbelieving, because if you do, you will fall away from the living God and perish forever.

2. As a means to protecting each other from such an evil

heart of unbelief speak sin-defeating, faith-sustaining words into each other's lives every day.

3. This warning and this exhortation is not because a person who truly belongs to Christ can be lost, but because perseverance is the evidence that you truly belong to Christ. If you fall away, you show that you never truly shared in Christ. And God will never let this happen to those who have shared in Christ.

8.3 God's Unbreakable Faithfulness

"Those whom he predestined he also called, and those whom he called he also justified, and those whom he justified he also glorified" (Romans 8:30). Which means: Between eternity past in God's predestination, and eternity future in God's glorification, none is lost. No one who is predestined for sonship fails to be called. And no one who is called fails to be justified. And no one who is justified fails to be glorified. This is an unbreakable steel chain of divine covenant faithfulness.

And so Paul says, "And I am sure of this, that he who began a good work in you will bring it to completion at the day of Jesus Christ" (Philippians 1:6). "He will sustain you to the end, guiltless in the day of our Lord Jesus Christ. God is faithful, by whom you were called into the fellowship of his Son, Jesus Christ our Lord" (1 Corinthians 1:8–9). These are the promises of our God who cannot lie. Those who are born again are as secure as God is faithful.

8.4 How Is Our Perseverance Connected to the Cross of Christ?

What is the connection between this security—this promised perseverance—and the cross of our Lord Jesus? Just before Jesus shed his blood for sinners, he lifted up the cup at the last supper and said in Luke 22:20, "This cup that is poured out for you is the new covenant in my blood." What that means is that the new covenant, promised most explicitly in Jeremiah 31 and 32, was secured and sealed by the blood of Jesus. The new covenant comes true because Jesus died to establish it.

And what does the new covenant secure for all who belong to Christ? *Perseverance in faith to the end.* Listen to Jeremiah 32:40, "I will make with them an everlasting covenant, that I will not turn away from doing good to them. *And I will put the fear of me in their hearts, that they may not turn from me.*" The everlasting covenant—the new covenant—includes the unbreakable promise: "*I will put the fear of me in their hearts, that they may not turn from me.*" They may not. They will not. Christ sealed this covenant with his blood. He purchased your perseverance.

If you are persevering in faith today, you owe it to the blood of Jesus. The Holy Spirit, who is working in you to preserve your faith, honors the purchase of Jesus. God the Spirit works in us what God the Son obtained for us. The Father planned it. Jesus bought it. The Spirit applies it—all of them—infallibly. God is totally committed to the eternal security of his blood-bought children.

8.5 The Necessity of Community in the Certainty of Security

This leads us now to this one point of application. God has united the certainty of security with the necessity of community. Hebrews 3:13, "Exhort *one another* every day, as long as it is called 'today,' that none of you may be hardened by the deceitfulness of sin." Eternal security is a community project. Or we can now say blood-bought eternal security is a blood-bought community project.

That may sound as though it were fragile, since our communal life is always imperfect. But it is not fragile. It is no more fragile than the sovereign ability of God to bring others into your life and to send you into theirs. God will sovereignly preserve all who belong to Christ. And he will do it through the faith-sustaining ministry of other believers.

If you are married it means that God—not man ("what God has joined together")—has already put you in households designed for this very thing—the daily faith-sustaining, sin-defeating ministry of the word to each other. Husbands and wives. Parents and children.

Let me give you some examples of what this means for husbands and wives.

For husbands:

› Love your wife sacrificially and cherish her as a reflection of the love of Christ for the church (Ephesians 5:25, 29). It will sustain her faith to see this.

› Be alert to and discern your wife's spiritual, emotional, relational, and physical needs, and make the effort to meet those needs—directly or indirectly (Hebrews 3:12–13; 1 Peter 3:7).

- Seek to build up your wife with biblical knowledge, through your own words, and by your encouragement and help in connecting her with the teaching ministries provided by the church (John 8:32; Ephesians 4:25-30).
- Encourage and help your wife engage in ministry at church and in the world (Proverbs 31:20; Ephesians 4:11-12; 1 Timothy 5:9–10).

For wives:

- Be alert to your husband's spiritual condition and pray earnestly for him (1 Samuel 25:1–35; Hebrews 3:12–13).
- Encourage your husband by affirming evidences of grace in his life (Romans 15:2; Ephesians 4:29; Hebrews 10:24–25). It will sustain his faith to hear this.
- Support him in all his leadership efforts, and be responsive to every effort he makes to lead spiritually (Ephesians 5:21–24; 1 Peter 3:1–6).
- Share from your life and your meditation the things God is teaching you about Christ and his ways (Romans 15:13–14; 1 Thessalonians 4:18).
- Join him in serious conversation with respect and wisdom (Proverbs 31:26; Romans 15:2; 1 Thessalonians 5:11).
- Suggest to him people and resources that may be of help

to him (Genesis 2:18; Proverbs 31:12; Acts 20:32). No one knows him like you know him.

- Humbly and hopefully help him be aware of unhelpful habits or sins you may see in his life (Hebrews 3:12–13; James 5:16). We are seeking to do Hebrews 3:13 for each other.

I know this assumes that you are both believers, and that you are both willing. And I know that's not true of every married couple. But it is what God calls us to pray toward and move toward for the sake of our spouses and our children's perseverance in faith. Eternal security is a family project.

8.6 There Is No Substitute for the Church

Here's a final word to all of us, to the single and the married. God did not design marriage to replace the church. He didn't design families to replace friendships. Every married man needs believing men in his life. Every married woman needs other believing women in her life. The young people need other young people. And single people need married people and single people in their lives. Families are not substitutes for any of these relationships.

The blood-bought church of Christ is the new, supernatural family. Single people, married people, old and young, rich and poor, every ethnicity find brothers and sisters here. Marriage is temporary. Parenting is temporary. But the church—the new family—is eternal.

H. MORE ABOUT PERSEVERANCE

Settling Our Security in God Alone

One obstacle to enjoying the security we have in Christ is the hard texts in the New Testament that seem to contradict it. Just when we start to feel that we are eternally secure in his love, along comes a passage of Scripture that threatens us and seems to rob us of security. And I don't think there will be any deep, abiding sense of security in God until we own up to these passages of Scripture and see how they relate to the assurance of God's love and power.

For example, consider this sampling from nine New Testament books.

1. Romans 11:20–21, "Unbelieving Israelites were broken off because of their unbelief, but you stand fast only through faith. So do not become proud but fear. For if God did not spare the natural branches, neither will he spare you."

2. 1 Corinthians 10:12, "Let anyone who thinks that he stands take heed lest he fall." Also 1 Corinthians 15:2, "I preached to you the gospel ... by which you are saved if you hold it fast—unless you believed in vain."

3. 2 Corinthians 13:5, "Examine yourself to see whether you are holding to your faith. Test yourselves. Do you not realize that Jesus Christ is in you—unless you fail to meet the test!"

4. Galatians 6:9, "Let us not grow weary in well-doing, for in due season we shall reap, if we do not lose heart."

5. Philippians 2:12, "Work out your salvation with fear and trembling."

6. Colossians 1:21–23, "You who were estranged... Christ has reconciled... in order to present you holy and blameless... provided that you continue in the faith, stable and steadfast, not shifting from the hope of the gospel."

7. Hebrews 12:14, "Strive for peace and for the holiness without which no one will see the Lord."

8. 1 Peter 1:17, "If you invoke as Father him who judges each one impartially according to his deeds, conduct yourselves with fear throughout the time of your exile."

9. Revelation 2:10, "Be faithful unto death and I will give you the crown of life."

Threatening Our Shallow Security

All of these passages above teach that the test of genuineness for the Christian is perseverance in faith and holiness of life. They warn us that the attempt to offer security apart from lasting faith and loving lives is perilous. To offer security without these indispensable realities is to offer security at the price of destruction.

But it would be a terrible misunderstanding if we thought that these Scriptures were written to threaten our security in God. Exactly the opposite is the case. *They are written to threaten our security in everything but God.* If you find your security in health, the Bible is a threat to you. If you find your security in your family or job or money or education, the Bible is a threat to you. And in threatening all these utterly inadequate foundations of security, the Bible drives us relentlessly and lovingly back to the one and only eternal and unshakable foundation for security—God. All the threats and warnings of the Bible declare with one voice: sin is an effort to feel secure in anything other than God.

Therefore, when God demands on the one hand, "Turn from sinning or you will die," and on the other hand, "Feel eternally secure in my love and you will live," he is not demanding two different things. Sin is what you do when you replace security in God with other things. So when God threatens our feelings of security in the world, it's because he wants us to feel secure in his love and power. The threats and promises of Scripture have one message: *seek your security in God alone.*

Security in God Alone

Ephesians 1:11–14 is one of the clearest statements in the Bible about God's desire that his people find their security in him alone, that we feel secure in his love and power.

> 11 *In him we have obtained an inheritance, having been predestined according to the purpose of him who works all things according to the counsel of his will,* 12 *so that we who were the first to hope in Christ might be to the praise of his glory.* 13 *In him you also, when you heard the word of truth, the gospel of your salvation, and believed in him, were sealed with the promised Holy Spirit,* 14 *who is the guarantee of our inheritance until we acquire possession of it, to the praise of his glory.*

The first and most important thing to see in these three verses is that they begin and end with God's ultimate purpose to glorify himself. Verse 12: "We were destined and appointed to live *for the praise of his glory.*" Verse 14: he has guaranteed our inheritance *to the praise of his glory.* The most basic fact you can say about the righteousness of God is that he has an unwavering commitment to his own glory. Everything he does, he does to heighten the intensity with which his people praise him for his glory.

The second thing to see is that the people whose inheritance God guarantees are the people who *believe* the gospel (verse 13). ("You who have believed were sealed.") There is a direct connection between believing God's Word and living for the praise of his glory. One of the greatest ways to honor people is to trust them. And since God is committed to his own honor above all things, therefore he is utterly committed to those who trust him.

Therefore, the third thing to see from this text is just what you would expect. Since God does all things for the praise of his glory, and since believing his word magnifies that glory, therefore God takes decisive steps to secure for himself the magnification of his glory forever: he *seals* the believer with the Holy Spirit, and *guarantees* that we will come to our inheritance praising his glory. God is so passionately committed to having a people for his own possession who live forever for the praise of his glory that he is not about to let our eternal destiny depend on our native powers of willing or doing. He commissions his Holy Spirit to enter our lives and to make us secure forever.

Sealed and Guaranteed, Forever

There are two great words here that aim to help us feel secure in God's love and power: the word "*sealed*," and the word "*guarantee*."

Let's see if we can unseal this word "sealed" and look inside. What does it mean that believers have been *sealed by the Holy Spirit* (verse 13)? The word is used at least three different ways in the New Testament.

1. In Matthew 27:66 the tomb of Jesus was secured by *sealing* it and putting guards around it. In Revelation 20:3 God throws Satan into a pit and *seals* it over so he can't escape. So one meaning is locking something up, closing it in.

2. Another way the word is used is found in Romans 4:11 where Abraham's circumcision is called the sign and *seal* of the righteousness he had by faith. And in 1 Corinthians 9:2 Paul says that his converts are the *seal* of his apostleship. So a second meaning of sealing is giving a sign of authenticity.

3. A third meaning of the word is found in Revelation 7:3 where the *seal* of God is put on the forehead of God's servants to protect them from the wrath coming upon the world.

So what did Paul mean in Ephesians 1:13 when he said that believers are sealed with the Holy Spirit? No matter which of these meanings you use the basic truth is the same.

1. If the Spirit *seals shut*, the point must be that he seals in faith and seals out unbelief and apostasy.

2. If the Spirit seals us as a *sign of authenticity*, then he is

that sign and it is the Spirit's work in our life which is God's trademark. Our eternal sonship is real and authentic if we have the Spirit. He is the sign of divine reality in our lives.

3. Or if the Spirit *marks us with God's seal*, he protects us from evil forces which won't dare to enter a person bearing the mark of God's own possession.

However you come at this message contained in this word "sealed," it is a message of safety and security in God's love and power. God sends the Holy Spirit as a preserving seal to lock in our faith, as an authenticating seal to validate our sonship, and as a protecting seal to keep out destructive forces. The point is that God wants us to feel secure and safe in his love and power.

The other word Paul uses to drive this home is the word "guarantee" in verse 14. "You were sealed with the promised Holy Spirit which is the *guarantee* of our inheritance." Noël and I ran out of gas recently at the intersection of 66th Street and Penn Avenue. I ran up the street to a nearby service station and borrowed a can with two dollars' worth of gas. I said I would be right back and buy 15 dollars' worth. But I had to leave my driver's license. Why? Because it was a *guarantee* I would come back and finish my business. They knew that my driver's license was valuable enough to me to give them a sense of security that I would come back with their can and pay for my gas.

So then, what is God saying to us when he gives us his Holy Spirit and calls him a guarantee or a down-payment?

He is saying, "My great desire for those who believe in me is that you feel secure in my love. I have chosen you before the foundation of the world. I have predestined you to be my children forever. I have redeemed you by the blood of my Son. And I have put my Spirit in you as a seal and a guarantee. Therefore, you will receive the inheritance and praise the glory of my grace forever and ever. And I tell you this here in Ephesians 1 because I want you to feel secure in my love and my power. I don't promise you an easy life. In fact, through many tribulations you must enter the kingdom. I don't promise always to speak in soft tones of approval, but to warn you in love whenever you begin to seek security in anything but me.

"Let me say it again: I have chosen you," says the Lord. "I have predestined you; I have redeemed you; I have sealed you by my Spirit. Your inheritance is sure, because I am passionately committed to magnify the glory of my grace in your salvation." God says to us:

> *When peace like a river attendeth* your *way,*
> *When sorrows like sea billows roll,*
> *Whatever* your *lot—I have taught you to say,*
> *It is well, it is well, with* your *soul.*

9. BIBLICAL MANHOOD AND WOMANHOOD

Then God said, "Let us make man in our image, after our likeness. And let them have dominion over the fish of the sea and over the birds of the heavens and over the livestock and over all the earth and over every creeping thing that creeps on the earth." [27] *So God created man in his own image, in the image of God he created him; male and female he created them.* [28] *And God blessed them. And God said to them, "Be fruitful and multiply and fill the earth and subdue it, and have dominion over the fish of the sea and over the birds of the heavens and over every living thing that moves on the earth."* [29] *And God said, "Behold, I have given you every plant yielding seed that is on the face of all the earth, and every tree with seed in its fruit. You shall have them for food.* [30] *And to every beast of the earth and to every bird of the heavens and to everything that creeps on*

the earth, everything that has the breath of life, I have given every green plant for food." And it was so. [31] *And God saw everything that he had made, and behold, it was very good. And there was evening and there was morning, the sixth day.*
—Genesis 1:26–31

9.1 What Does "Complementarian" Mean?

One of the thirty-year theological trademarks of Bethlehem is the way we understand God's purposes for how men and women relate to each other in family and church and society. If you want a name to put a name on this understanding, we would say we are complementarian—based on the word "complement." In other words, we believe that when it comes to human sexuality, the greatest display of God's glory, and the greatest joy of human relationships, and the greatest fruitfulness in ministry come about when the deep differences between men and women are embraced and celebrated as complements to each other. They complete and beautify each other.

The intention with the word "complementarian" is to locate our way of life between two kinds of error: on the one side would be the abuses of women under male domination, and on the other side would be the negation of gender differences where they have beautiful significance.

This means that, on the one hand, complementarians acknowledge and lament the history of abuses of women personally and systemically, and the present evils globally and locally in the exploitation and diminishing of women and girls. And, on the other hand, complementarians lament the feminist and egalitarian impulses that minimize God-given differences between men and women and dismantle the order God has designed for the flourishing of our life together.

So complementarians resist the impulses of a chauvinistic, dominating, and abusive culture, one the one side, and the impulses of a sex-blind, gender-leveling, unisex culture, on the other side. And we take our stand between these two ways of life not because the middle ground is a safe place (it is emphatically not), but because we think this is the good plan of God in the Bible for men and women. "Very good," as he says in Genesis 1.

In fact, I would say that the attempt by feminism to remedy the male abuse of women by nullifying gender differences, backfires and produces millions of men that women cannot enjoy because of their unmanliness, or cannot endure because of their distorted, brutal manliness. In other words, if we don't teach boys and girls about the truth and beauty and value of their differences, and how to live them out, those differences do not mature in healthy ways but dysfunctional ways. And a generation of young adults comes into being who simply do not know what it means to be a mature man or a woman; and the cultural price we pay for that is enormous.

The way I would like to approach this is move from the general to the specific: a word about being human, an illustration about being male and female, and then a specific text to show the biblical roots.

9.2 The Wonder of Being Human

Let me start by saying a word about being human. My first Sunday at Bethlehem, July 13, 1980 in the evening I gave a message titled "Life Is Not Trivial." In it I said,

> *Every human being now and then feels a longing that life not dribble away like a leaky faucet. You've all tasted the desire that day-to-day life be more than a series of trifles. It can happen when you are reading a poem, when you are kneeling in your closet, when you are standing by the lakeside at sunset. It very often happens at birth and death.*

I quoted Moses from Deuteronomy 32:46, "Lay to heart all the words which I enjoin upon you this day, that you may command them to your children, that they may be careful to do all the words of this law. For *it is no trifle* for you but it is your life."

Deep in every God-created human being, bearing the insignia of humanity in the image of God, there is a longing for life, not to be meaningless. Not be trivial, frivolous, inconsequential. I recently read this quote from the crime novelist, Agatha Christie (1896–1976),

> *I like living. I have sometimes been wildly, despairingly, acutely miserable, racked with sorrow, but through it all, I still know quite certainly, that just to be alive, is a grand thing.*

I think this is wonderfully true. To be a living human being is a grand thing. Haven't you all had those rare and wonderful moments when you are standing by a window, or door, or anywhere, and suddenly, unbidden, and powerful comes the awakening: *I am alive. I am alive. Not like a tree or rabbit, but like a human being. I am thinking, feeling, longing, regretting, grieving. Alive. Made in the very image of God. And this is a grand thing.*

It is a grand thing. And part of the grandeur of being a living human being created in the image of God is that you are either male or female. "God created man in his own image, in the image of God he created him; male and female he created them" (Genesis 1:27). Nobody is a generic human being. There is no such thing. God never intended that there be. God creates male human beings and female human beings. And this is a grand thing.

It is a travesty of these human natures to think God's only design in the differences was for making and nursing babies. The differences are too many and too deep for such a superficial explanation. A woman is a woman to the depths of her humanity. And a man is a man to the depths of his humanity. And this is a grand thing. So my first point is that God has done a grand thing in making us male and female in his image. Don't diminish this. Delight in it. Glory in being alive as the male or female person you are.

9.3 Gender Roles Are Not About Competency

Let me create an illustration to portray some of the differences between manhood and womanhood. A picture may be worth a thousand words—even a word picture.

Suppose among the young adults at the Downtown Campus a young man and woman, say 20-years old, find themselves chatting before the worship service. He likes what he hears and sees, and says, "Are you sitting with anyone?" They sit together. They notice how each other engage with God in worship.

When the service is over, as they are leaving, he says, "Do you have any lunch plans? I'd love to treat you to lunch." At that point she can signal she is not interested, "I do have some plans. But thanks." Or she can signal the opposite: "I do, but let me make a call. I think I can change them. I'd love to go."

Neither has a car, so he suggests they walk to Maria's Café down on Franklin Avenue, about 10 minutes from the church. As they walk he finds out that she has a black belt in martial arts, and that she is one of the best in the state. At 19th Street two men block their way ominously and say, "Pretty girlfriend you've got there. We'd like her purse and your wallet. In fact, she's so pretty we'd like her."

The thought goes through his head: "She can whip these guys." But instead of stepping behind her, he takes her arm, pulls her back behind him, and says, "If you're going to touch her, it will be over my dead body."

When they make their move, he tackles them both and tells her to run. They knock him unconscious, but before they know what hit them, she has put them both on their backs with their teeth knocked out. And a little crowd has gathered. The police and ambulance come and she gets in the ambulance with the young man just regaining his consciousness. And she has one main thought on the way to the hospital: *This is the kind of man I want to marry.*

The main point of that story is to illustrate that the deeper differences of manhood and womanhood are not superior or inferior competences. There are rather deep dispositions or inclinations written on the heart, albeit often very distorted. Notice three crucial things.

First, he took the initiative and asked if he could sit with her and if she would go to lunch and suggested the place and how to get there. She saw clearly what he was doing, and responded freely according to her desires. She joined the dance. This says nothing about who has superior competences in planning. God writes the impulse to lead on a man's heart, and the wisdom to discern it and enjoy it on a woman's heart.

Second, he said that he wanted to treat her to lunch. He's paying. This sends a signal from the young man: "I think that's part of my responsibility. In this little drama of life, I initiate, I provide." She understands and approves. She supports the initiative and graciously accepts the offer to be provided for. She takes the next step in the choreography. And it says nothing about who is wealthier or more capable of earning. It is what God's man feels he must do.

Third, it is irrelevant to the masculine soul that a woman he is with has greater self-defending competencies. It is his deep, God-given, masculine impulse to protect her. It is not a matter of superior competency. It is a matter of manhood. She saw it. She did not feel belittled by it, but honored, and she loved it.

At the heart of mature manhood is the God-given sense (disposition, inclination) that the primary responsibility (not sole responsibility) lies with him when it comes to leadership-initiative, provision, and protection. And at the heart of mature womanhood is the God-given sense (disposition, inclination) that none of this implies her inferiority, but that it will be a beautiful thing to come alongside such a man and gladly affirm and receive this kind of leadership and provision and protection.

9.4 The Testimony and Application of Ephesians 5:22–33

For those who disagree with this complementarian view, the likely criticism would be that it is all culturally determined. "It's not innate and it's not from God." Complementarians, they would say, are just reflecting the home they grew up in and the biases of their childhood.

Now that's possible. Everyone brings assumptions and preferences to this issue. The question is: "Does God reveal his will about these things in his word?"

Let's look first at a biblical text dealing with marriage and then one dealing very briefly with the church. In both texts, Christ-like, humble, loving, sacrificial men are to take primary responsibility for leadership, provision and protection. And women are called to come alongside these men, support that leadership, and advance the kingdom of Christ with the full range of her gifts in the paths laid out in Scripture.

First, a text on marriage and the home. Ephesians 5:22–33,

> *Wives, submit to your own husbands, as to the Lord.* 23 *For the husband is the head of the wife even as Christ is the head of the church, his body, and is himself its Savior.* 24 *Now as the church submits to Christ, so also wives should submit in everything to their*

husbands. 25 *Husbands, love your wives, as Christ loved the church and gave himself up for her,* 26 *that he might sanctify her, having cleansed her by the washing of water with the word,* 27 *so that he might present the church to himself in splendor, without spot or wrinkle or any such thing, that she might be holy and without blemish.* 28 *In the same way husbands should love their wives as their own bodies. He who loves his wife loves himself.* 29 *For no one ever hated his own flesh, but nourishes and cherishes it, just as Christ does the church,* 30 *because we are members of his body. [Then, quoting Genesis 2:24]* 31 *"Therefore a man shall leave his father and mother and hold fast to his wife, and the two shall become one flesh."* 32 *This mystery is profound, and I am saying that it refers to Christ and the church.* 33 *However, let each one of you love his wife as himself, and let the wife see that she respects her husband.*

Here are four observations in this text:

› Marriage is a dramatization of Christ's relationship to his church. Verse 32: "This mystery is profound, and I am saying that it refers to Christ and the church."

› In this drama, the husband takes his cues from Christ and the wife takes her cues from God's will for the church. Verse 25: "Husbands, love your wives, as Christ loved the church and gave himself up for her." Verse 22: "Wives, submit to your own husbands, as to the Lord. For the husband is the head of the wife even as Christ is the head of the church."

- So the primary responsibility for initiative and leadership in the home is to come from the husband who is taking his cues from Christ, the head. And it is clear that this is not about rights and power, but about responsibility and sacrifice. Verse 25: "As Christ loved the church and gave himself for her." No abuse. No bossiness. No authoritarianism. No arrogance. Here is a man whose pride has been broken by his own need for a Savior, and he is willing to bear the burden of leadership given to him by his Master, no matter how heavy the load. Godly women see this and are glad.
- This leadership in the home involves the sense of primary responsibility for nourishing provision and tender protection. Verse 29: "For no one ever hated his own flesh (that is, his wife), but nourishes and cherishes it, just as Christ does the church." The word, "nourishes" implies nourishing provision. And the word "cherishes" implies tender protection. This is what Christ does for his bride. This is what the godly husband feels the primary responsibility to do for his wife and family.

So a complementarian concludes that biblical headship for the husband is the divine calling to take primary responsibility for Christlike servant-leadership, protection and provision in the home. And biblical submission for the wife is the divine calling to honor and affirm her husband's leadership and help carry it through according to her gifts. "A helper suitable for him," as Genesis 2:18 says.

We don't have time to develop the arguments for how this applies to the church. So I will just make

> *some summary comments so you can know how we as complementarians see it. In 1 Timothy 2:12 Paul says, "I do not permit a woman to teach or to exercise authority over a man." In the context we take that to mean: the primary responsibility for governance and teaching in the church should be carried by spiritual men. These are the two functions that distinguish elders from deacons: governing (1 Timothy 5:17) and teaching (1 Timothy 3:2). So the clearest way we apply this passage is to say that the elders of the church should be spiritual men.*

In other words, since the church is the family of God, the realities of headship and submission that we saw in marriage (Ephesians 5:22–33) have their counterparts in the church.

› "Authority" (in 1 Timothy 2:12) refers to the divine calling of spiritual, gifted men to take primary responsibility as elders for Christlike, servant-leadership and teaching in the church.

› And "submission" refers to the divine calling of the rest of the church, both men and women, to honor and affirm the leadership and teaching of the elders and to be equipped by them for the hundreds and hundreds of various ministries available to men and women in the service of Christ.

That last point is very important. For men and women who have a heart to minister—to save souls and heal broken lives and resist evil and meet needs—there are fields of opportunity that are simply endless. God intends for the entire church to be mobilized in ministry, male and female. Nobody is to simply stay at home watching soaps and ballgames while the world burns.

9.5 A Specific Challenge to Men

The biblical picture of manhood and womanhood is a call for men and women to realize it is a grand thing to be a man created in the image of God, and it is an equally grand thing to be a woman created in the image of God. But since the burden of primary responsibility lies on the men—let me challenge them mainly.

Men, do you have a moral vision for your families, a zeal for the house of the Lord, a magnificent commitment to the advancement of the kingdom, an articulate dream for the mission of the church and a tenderhearted tenacity to make it real? You can't lead a godly woman without this. She is a grand being!

There are hundreds of such men in the church today. And more are needed. When the Lord visits his church and creates a mighty army of deeply spiritual, humble, strong, Christlike men committed to the word of God and the mission of the church, the vast army of women will rejoice over the leadership of these men and enter into a joyful partnership. And that will be a grand thing.

I. MORE ABOUT BIBLICAL MANHOOD AND WOMANHOOD

Conflict and Confusion After the Fall

God created us in his image as male and female. This

implies six important things: 1) equality of personhood, 2) equality of dignity, 3) mutual respect, 4) harmony, 5) complementarity, and 6) a unified destiny.

1. Equality of Personhood

Equality of personhood means that a man is not less a person than a woman because he has hair on his chest like a gorilla, and woman is not less a person because she has no hair on her chest like a fish. They are equal in their personhood and their differences don't change that basic truth.

2. Equality of Dignity

Equality of dignity means that they are to be equally honored as humans in the image of God. Peter says (in 1 Peter 2:17), "honor all," that is, all humans. There is an honor to be paid to persons simply because they are humans. There is even an honor that we owe to the most despicable of criminals just because they are human and not a dog. And that honor belongs to male and female equally.

3. Mutual Respect

Mutual respect means that men and women should be equally zealous to respect and honor each other. Respect should never flow just one direction. Created in the image of God, male and female should look at each other with a kind of awe—an awe that is tainted but not destroyed by sin.

4. Harmony

Harmony means that there should be peaceful cooperation

between men and women. We should find ways to oil the gears of our relationships so that there is teamwork and rapport and mutual helpfulness and joy.

5. Complementarity

Complementarity means that the music of our relationships should not be merely the sound of singing in unison. It should be the integrated sound of soprano and bass, alto and tenor. It means that the differences of male and female will be respected and affirmed and valued. It means that male and female will not try to duplicate each other, but will highlight in each other the unique qualities that make for mutual enrichment.

6. Unified Destiny

Unified destiny means that male and female, when they come to faith in Christ, are "fellow heirs of the grace of life" (1 Peter 3:7). We are destined for an equal enjoyment of the revelation of the glory of God in the age to come.

So in creating human beings as male and female in his image, God had something wonderful in mind. He still has it in mind. And in Jesus Christ he means to redeem this vision from the ravages of sin.

Understanding the Curse

I want you to sense very keenly what the conflict is between men and women and how great the confusion is today about what it means to be a man or a woman.

Let's look at Genesis 3:16. Adam and Eve have both

sinned against God. They have distrusted his goodness and turned away from him to depend on their own wisdom for how to be happy. So they rejected his word and they ate the fruit of the tree of the knowledge of good and evil. God calls them to account and now describes to them what the curse will be on human life because of sin. In Genesis 3:16 God says to the woman, "I will greatly multiply your pain in childbearing; in pain you shall bring forth children, and your desire shall be for your husband, and he shall rule over you."

This is a description of the curse. It is a description of misery, not a model for marriage. This is the way it's going to be in history where sin has the upper hand. But what is really being said here? What is the nature of this ruined relationship after sin?

The key comes from recognizing the connection between the last words of this verse (3:16b) and the last words of Genesis 4:7. Here God is warning Cain about his resentment and anger against Abel. God tells him that sin is about to get the upper hand in his life. Notice at the end of the verse 7: "Sin is crouching at the door; its desire is for you, but you must master it [literally: you shall rule over it]."

The parallel here between 3:16 and 4:7 is amazingly close. The words are virtually the same in Hebrew, but you can see this in the English as well. In 3:16 God says to the woman, "Your desire is for your husband, and he shall rule over you." In 4:7 God says to Cain, "Sin's desire is for you, and you shall rule over it."

Now the reason this is important to see is that it shows us more clearly what is meant by "desire." When 4:7 says that sin is crouching at the door of Cain's heart (like a lion,

Genesis 49:9) and that its desire is for him, it means that sin wants to overpower him. It wants to defeat him and subdue him and make him the slave of sin.

Now when we go back to 3:16, we should probably see the same meaning in the sinful desire of woman. When it says, "Your desire shall be for your husband," it means that when sin has the upper hand in woman, she will desire to overpower or subdue or exploit man. And when sin has the upper hand in man, he will respond in like manner and with his strength subdue her, or rule over her.

So what is really described in the curse of 3:16 is the ugly conflict between the male and female that has marked so much of human history. Maleness as God created it has been depraved and corrupted by sin. Femaleness as God created it has been depraved and corrupted by sin. The essence of sin is self-reliance and self-exaltation. First in rebellion against God, and then in exploitation of each other.

So the essence of corrupted maleness is the self-aggrandizing effort to subdue and control and exploit women for its own private desires. And the essence of corrupted femaleness is the self-aggrandizing effort to subdue and control and exploit men for its own private desires. And the difference is found mainly in the different weaknesses that we can exploit in one another.

As a rule, men have more brute strength than women and so they can rape and abuse and threaten and sit around and snap their finger. It's fashionable to say those sorts of things today. But it's just as true that women are sinners. We are in God's image, male and female; and we are depraved, male and female. Women may not have as much brute strength as men, but she knows ways to subdue him. She can very often run circles around him with her words and where her words fail, she knows the weakness of his lust.

If you have any doubts about the power of sinful woman to control sinful man, just reflect for a moment on the number one marketing force in the world—the female body. She can sell anything because she knows the universal weakness of man and how to control him with it. The exploitation of women by sinful men is conspicuous because it is often harsh and violent. But a moment's reflection will show you that the exploitation of men by sinful women is just as pervasive in our society. The difference is that our sinful society sanctions the one perversity and not the other. (There are societies that do just the opposite.)

Different Movements in a Marvelous Dance

This is not the way God meant it to be before sin, when man and woman were dependent on him for how to live. This is the result of rebellion against God. How, then, did God mean it to be? What was the relationship between Adam and Eve supposed to look like before sin entered the world?

We've seen part of the answer: they were created in the image of God according to Genesis 1:27 and so the relationship they have was supposed to be governed by equality of personhood, equality of dignity, mutual respect, harmony, complementarity, and a unified destiny.

But that's only part of the answer.

It's like saying to a man and woman ballet dancer: "Remember, you are both equally accomplished dancers; you are equally regarded among your peers; you must seek harmonious execution; you must complement each other's moves; and don't forget you will share the applause together."

That kind of counsel is very important and will deeply affect the beauty of the performance. But if that's all they know about the dance they're about to perform, they won't be able to do it. *They have to know the movements.* They have to know their different positions. They have to know who will fall and who will catch. Who will run and who will stand. It is of the very essence of dance and drama that the players know the distinct movements they must make.

If they don't know their different assignments on the stage, there will be no drama, no dance.

10. SORROWFUL YET ALWAYS REJOICING

We are ambassadors for Christ, God making his appeal through us. We implore you on behalf of Christ, be reconciled to God. [21] *For our sake he made him to be sin who knew no sin, so that in him we might become the righteousness of God.* [1] *Working together with him, then, we appeal to you not to receive the grace of God in vain.* [2] *For he says, "In a favorable time I listened to you, and in a day of salvation I have helped you." Behold, now is the favorable time; behold, now is the day of salvation.* [3] *We put no obstacle in anyone's way, so that no fault may be found with our ministry,* [4] *but as servants of God we commend ourselves in every way: by great endurance, in afflictions, hardships, calamities,* [5] *beatings, imprisonments, riots, labors, sleepless nights, hunger;* [6] *by purity, knowledge, patience, kindness, the Holy Spirit, genuine love;* [7] *by truthful speech, and the power of God; with the weapons of righteousness for the right hand and for the left;* [8] *through honor and dishonor, through slander and praise. We are treated as impostors, and yet are true;* [9] *as unknown, and yet well known; as dying, and behold, we live; as punished, and yet not killed;* [10] *as sorrowful, yet always rejoicing; as poor, yet making many rich; as having nothing, yet possessing everything.* [11] *We have spoken freely to you, Corinthians; our heart is wide open.* [12] *You are not restricted by us, but you are restricted in your own affections.* [13] *In return (I speak as to children) widen your hearts also.* —2 Corinthians 5:20–6:13

Let me tell you here at the very beginning the main point of this chapter. It is this:

> *What the world needs from the church is our indomitable joy in Jesus in the midst of suffering and sorrow.*

10.1 What the World Needs to See in Us

I have tried these thirty-two-and-a-half years to lead the staff and the elders and all of Bethlehem in the experience of sorrowful yet always rejoicing. I turn with dismay from church services that are treated like radio talk shows where everything sounds like chipper, frisky, high-spirited chatter designed to make people feel lighthearted and playful and bouncy. I look at those services and say to myself: "Don't you know that people are sitting out there who are dying of cancer, whose marriage is a living hell, whose children have broken their hearts, who are barely making it financially, who have just lost their job, who are lonely and frightened and misunderstood and depressed? And you are going to try to create an atmosphere of bouncy, chipper, frisky, light-hearted, playful worship?"

And, of course, there will be those who hear me say that and say: "Oh, so you think what those people need is a morose, gloomy, sullen, dark, heavy atmosphere of solemnity?"

No. What they need is to see and feel indomitable joy in Jesus in the midst of suffering and sorrow. "Sorrowful, yet always rejoicing." They need to taste that these church people are not playing games here. They are not using religion as a platform for the same-old, hyped-up self-help that the world offers every day. They need the greatness and the grandeur of God over their heads like galaxies of hope. They need the unfathomable crucified and risen Christ embracing them in love with blood all over his face and hands. And they need the thousand-mile-deep rock of God's word under their feet. They need to hear us sing with all our heart and soul,

Ye fearful saints, fresh courage take;
The clouds ye so much dread
Are big with mercy and shall break
In blessings on your head.
His purposes will ripen fast,
Unfolding every hour;
The bud may have a bitter taste,
But sweet will be the flower.

They need to hear the indomitable joy in sorrow as we sing:

His oath, His covenant, His blood,
Support me in the whelming flood.
When all around my soul gives way,
He then is all my Hope and Stay.

If you ask me, "Doesn't the world need to see Christians as happy in order to know the truth of our faith and be drawn to the great Savior?" My answer is: "Yes, yes, yes." And they need to see that our happiness is the indomitable work of Christ in the midst of our sorrow—a sorrow probably deeper than they have ever known that we live with every day. They need to see "sorrowful, yet always rejoicing."

So let's put some of that rock under our feet now—the rock of God's word. Let's go to the Bible and see if these things are so.

10.2 Why Does It Matter What the World Needs?

We will focus on 2 Corinthians 6:3–10. Why have I put the emphasis on what the world needs? Why have I framed the main point of this sermon as: "What the world needs from the church is our indomitable joy in Jesus in the midst of suffering and sorrow?" The answer is in verses 3 and 4. Paul says, "We put no obstacle in anyone's way, so that no fault may be found with our ministry, but as servants of God we commend ourselves in every way."

In other words, Paul is saying: "What I am about to do in this chapter is remove obstacles and commend our ministry—our life and message." He wants the church in Corinth, and the world, not to write him off, not to walk away, not to misunderstand who he is and what he teaches and whom he represents. He wants to win them. If you want to use the language of seeker-friendly, watch how he does it.

It's amazing what he does here. Many savvy, church-growth communicators today would have no categories for this way of removing obstacles and commending Christianity. In fact, some might say: "Paul, you are not removing obstacles, you are creating obstacles."

So let's watch Paul remove obstacles and commend his ministry. This, he says in effect, is what the world needs.

He does this in three steps: 1) he describes the sufferings he endures; 2) he describes the character he tries to show; and 3) he describes the paradoxes of the Christian life.

10.3 Removing Obstacles in Three Steps

First, he describes the sufferings he endures for Christ (2 Corinthians 6:3–5):

> *We put no obstacle in anyone's way, so that no fault may be found with our ministry, but as servants of God we commend ourselves in every way: by great endurance, in afflictions, hardships, calamities, beatings, imprisonments, riots, labors, sleepless nights, hunger.*

So you may be asking yourself: "How is this removing obstacles? How is this commending his ministry? Why is this not putting people off rather than drawing them in?"

Second, he describes the character he tries to show (2 Corinthians 6:6–7):

> *... by purity, knowledge, patience, kindness, the Holy Spirit, genuine love; by truthful speech, and the*

power of God; with the weapons of righteousness for the right hand and for the left [probably the sword of the Spirit in the right hand and the shield of faith in the left, Ephesians 6:16–17].

So instead of being embittered and frustrated and angry and resentful by all the afflictions and hardships and calamities and labors and sleepless nights, by God's grace, Paul has shown patience and kindness and love. His spirit has not been broken by the pain of his ministry. In the Holy Spirit, he has found resources to give and not to grumble. To be patient in God's timing, rather than pity himself. To be kind to people, rather than take it out on others.

And third, Paul describes the paradoxes of the Christian life (2 Corinthians 6:8–10):

> *... through honor and dishonor, through slander and praise. We are treated as impostors, and yet are true; as unknown, and yet well known; as dying, and behold, we live; as punished, and yet not killed; as sorrowful, yet always rejoicing; as poor, yet making many rich; as having nothing, yet possessing everything.*

When you walk in the light and minister in the power of Holy Spirit, and speak the truth in "purity, knowledge, patience, kindness, and love," some people will honor you and some will dishonor you (verse 8a); some will slander you, and some will praise you (verse 8b). And that dishonor and slander may come in the form of calling you an imposter (verse 8c). "You're not real. You're just a religious hypocrite."

Remember Jesus said, "Woe to you, when all people speak well of you, for so their fathers did to the false prophets" (Luke 6:26). Which means that in Paul's mind a mixed reception (some honoring and praising, some dishonoring and slandering) was part of his commendation. It removed the obstacle that says, "You can't be a true prophet, all speak well of you."

10.4 Six Amazing Paradoxes in Gospel Ministry

Then come six more paradoxes. If you aren't careful, you might take these to mean that Paul is correcting false perceptions of Christians, but it's not quite like that. Every perception here of the outsider has truth in it. But Paul says, "What you see is true, but it's not the whole truth or the main truth."

Verse 9a: You see us "as unknown, and yet [we are] well known." *Yes, we are nobodies in the Roman empire, a tiny movement following a crucified and risen king. But oh we are known by God, and that is what counts* (1 Corinthians 8:3; Galatians 4:9).

Verse 9b: You see us "as dying, and behold, we live." *Yes, we die every day. We are crucified with Christ. Some of us are imprisoned and killed. But oh we live because Christ is our life now, and he will raise us from the dead.*

Verse 9c: You see us "as punished, and yet [we are] not killed." *Yes, we endure many human punishments and many divine chastenings, but over and over God has spared us from death. And he will spare us till our work is done.*

Verse 10a: You see us "as sorrowful, yet [we are] always rejoicing." *Yes, we are sorrowful. There are countless reasons for our hearts to break. But in them all we do not cease to rejoice, one of the greatest paradoxes of the Christian life!*

Verse 10b: You see us "as poor, yet [we are] making many rich." Yes, we are poor in this world's wealth. But we don't live to get rich on things, we live to make people rich on Jesus.

Verse 10c: You see us "as having nothing, yet [we are] possessing everything." In one sense, we have counted everything as loss or the surpassing value of knowing Christ Jesus (Philippians 3:8). But, in fact, we are children of God, and if children, then heirs of God and fellow heirs with Christ (Romans 8:17). To every Christian, Paul says, "All things are yours, whether Paul or Apollos or Cephas or the world or life or death or the present or the future—all are yours, and you are Christ's, and Christ is God's" (1 Corinthians 3:21–23).

10.5 Prosperity Does Not Commend Us

Now step back and remember what Paul said in verse 3: "We put no obstacle in anyone's way, so that no fault may be found with our ministry, but as servants of God we commend ourselves in every way." He has been removing obstacles to faith and commending the truth and value of his ministry—his life, his message, his Lord. And he has done it in exactly the opposite way that "the prosperity gospel" does it.

What obstacle has he removed? He has removed the obstacle that someone might think Paul is in the ministry for money, or for earthly comfort and ease. He has given every evidence he could to show that he is not a

Christian—and he is not in the ministry—for the worldly benefits it can bring. But there are many pastors today who think just the opposite about this. They think that having a lavish house and a lavish car and lavish clothes commend their ministry. That's simply not the way Paul thought. He thought that such things were obstacles.

Why? Because if they would entice anyone to Christ, it would be for the wrong reason. It would be because they think Jesus makes people rich and makes life comfortable and easy. No one should come to Christ for that reason. Enticing people to Christ with prosperous lifestyles and with chipper, bouncy, light-hearted, playful, superficial banter, posing as joy in Christ, will attract certain people, but not because Christ is seen in his glory and the Christian life is presented as the Calvary Road. Many false conversions happen this way.

So how is Paul commending his ministry, his life, his message, his Lord?

Verse 4: "As servants of God we commend ourselves in every way." How? By showing that knowing Christ, being known by Christ, having eternal life with Christ is better than all earthly wealth and prosperity and comfort. We commend our life and ministry by afflictions. We commend our life and ministry by calamities. We commend our life and ministry by sleepless nights. What does that mean? It means Christ is real to us, and Christ is infinitely precious, more to be desired than any wealth or comfort in this world. This is our commendation: *When all around our soul gives way he then is all our hope and stay.*

10.6 Two Pictures of Sorrowful Yet Always Rejoicing

What does it mean (verse 10) that part of Paul's commendation to the world is that he was sorrowful yet always rejoicing? It means that what the world needs from the church is our indomitable joy in Jesus in the midst of suffering and sorrow.

Let me move toward a close with two pictures of this sorrowful yet always rejoicing. One from Jesus and one from Paul.

When Jesus said in Matthew 5:11–12, "Blessed are you when others revile you and persecute you and utter all kinds of evil against you falsely on my account. Rejoice and be glad, for your reward is great in heaven," do you think it is random that the next thing he said was, "You are the salt of the earth... You are the light of the world?"

I don't think it was random. I think the tang of the salt that the world needs to taste, and the brightness of the light that the world needs to see is precisely this indomitable joy in the midst of sorrow.

Joy in the midst of health? Joy in the midst of wealth and ease? And when everyone speaks well of you? Why would that mean anything to the world? The world has that already. But indomitable joy in the midst of sorrow—that they do not have. That is what Jesus came to give in this fallen, pain-filled, sin-wracked world.

Or consider Paul's experience of agony over the lostness of his Jewish kinsmen in Romans 9:2–3. Remember Paul is the one who said in Philippians 4:4, "Rejoice in the Lord always; again I will say, rejoice." But in Romans 9:2–3, he writes, "I have great sorrow and unceasing anguish in my heart. For I could wish that I myself were accursed and cut off from Christ for the sake of my brothers, my kinsmen according to the flesh."

Don't miss the terrible burden of the word "unceasing" in verse 2. "I have great sorrow and unceasing anguish in my heart" because my kinsmen are perishing in unbelief cut off from the Messiah. Is Paul disobeying his own command to rejoice always? No. Because he said in 2 Corinthians 6:10, "We are sorrowful yet always rejoicing."

10.7 Salt and Light in This World

Is this not what the world needs from us? Picture yourself sitting across the table at your favorite restaurant from someone you care about very much who is not a believer. You have shared the gospel before, and they have been unresponsive. God gives you the grace this time to plead with them. And he gives you the grace of tears. And you say:

> *I want so bad for you to believe and be a follower of Jesus with me. I want you to have eternal life. I want us to be with Christ forever together. I want you to share the joy of knowing your sins are forgiven and that Jesus is your friend. And I can hardly bear the thought of losing you. It feels like a heavy stone in my chest.*

Isn't that what the world needs from us? Not just an invitation to joy, not just a painful expression of concern, but the pain and the joy coming together in such a way that they have never seen anything like this. They have never been loved like this. They have never seen indomitable joy in Jesus in the midst of sorrow. And by God's grace, it may taste like the salt of the earth and look like the light of the world. So I say one last time:

> *What the world needs from the church—from us—is our indomitable joy in Jesus in the midst of suffering and sorrow.*

This was Paul's commendation of his ministry. May it be our commendation of Christ. It is no accident that Paul concluded the greatest chapter in the Bible—Romans 8—with words that are designed pointedly to sustain your joy and my joy in the face of suffering and loss:

> *What then shall we say to these things? If God is for us, who can be against us? He who did not spare his own Son but gave him up for us all, how will he not also with him graciously give us all things? Who shall bring any charge against God's elect? It is God who justifies. Who is to condemn? Christ Jesus is the one who died—more than that, who was raised—who is at the right hand of God, who indeed is interceding for us. Who shall separate us from the love of Christ? Shall tribulation, or distress, or persecution, or famine, or nakedness, or danger, or sword? As it is written, "For your sake we are being killed all the day long; we are regarded as sheep to be slaughtered." No, in [not instead of, but in!] all these things we are more than conquerors through him who loved us. For I am sure that neither death nor life, nor angels nor rulers, nor things present nor*

> *things to come, nor powers, nor height nor depth, nor anything else in all creation, will be able to separate us from the love of God in Christ Jesus our Lord.*
> —Romans 8:31–39

So, Christian, let the world taste your indomitable joy in suffering and sorrow.

J. MORE ABOUT SUFFERING

Six Reasons to Keep on Rejoicing No Matter What

> *Beloved, do not be surprised at the fiery trial when it comes upon you to test you, as though something strange were happening to you. But rejoice insofar as you share Christ's sufferings, that you may also rejoice and be glad when his glory is revealed.*
> —1 Peter 4:12–13

The command is found in verse 13: "Rejoice insofar as you share Christ's sufferings." Keep on rejoicing. When you are thrown in the cellars of suffering, keep on rejoicing. When you dive in the sea of affliction, keep on rejoicing. In fact, keep on rejoicing not in spite of the affliction but even because of it. This is not a little piece of advice about the power of positive thinking. This is an utterly radical, abnormal, supernatural way to respond to suffering. It is not in our power. It is not for the sake of our honor. It is the way spiritual aliens and exiles live on the earth for the glory of the great King.

"Count it all joy when you meet various trials," is foolish advice, except for one thing—God. Peter gives six reasons why we can "keep on rejoicing" when the suffering comes. They all relate to God.

1. Not a Surprise but a Plan

Keep on rejoicing because the suffering is not a surprise but a plan.

Verse 12: "Beloved, do not be surprised at the fiery trial when it comes upon you to test you, as though something strange were happening to you." It isn't strange. It isn't absurd. It isn't meaningless. It is purposeful. It is for your testing. Look at verse 19: "Let those who suffer according to God's will entrust their souls to a faithful Creator." "According to God's will." Suffering is not outside the will of God. It is in God's will. This is true even when Satan may be the immediate cause. God is sovereign over all things, including our suffering, and including Satan.

By why? For what purpose? Compare verses 12 and 17. Verse 12: your fiery ordeal comes "for your testing." Verse 17 says, "For it is time for judgment to begin at the household of God; and if it begins with us, what will be the outcome for those who do not obey the gospel of God?" The point is that God's judgment is moving through the earth. The church does not escape. When the fire of judgment burns the church, it is a testing, proving, purifying fire. When it burns the world, it either awakens or destroys.

Verse 18: "If the righteous is scarcely saved, what will become of the ungodly and the sinner?" Believers pass through the testing fire of God's judgment—not because he hates us, but because he loves us and wills our purity. God hates sin so much and loves his children so much that he will spare us no pain to rid us of what he hates.

So reason number one is that suffering is not surprising; it is planned. It is a testing. It is purifying fire. It proves and strengthens real faith, and it consumes "performance faith."

Alexander Solzhenitsyn had long been impressed with the patience and longsuffering of Russian believers. One night in prison in Siberia Boris Kornfeld, a Jewish doctor, sat up with Solzhenitsyn and told him the story of his conversion to Christ. The same night Kornfeld was clubbed to death. Solzhenitsyn said that Kornfeld's last words were, "lay upon me as an inheritance . . . It was only when I lay there on rotting prison straw that I sensed within myself the first stirrings of good... Bless you, prison, for having been my life."

We have strong hope, therefore, that the sufferings of our own day will bring purity and life to many. Suffering is not surprising; it is purposeful.

2. Evidence of Union with Christ

Keep on rejoicing because your suffering as a Christian is an evidence of your union with Christ.

Verse 13: "But rejoice insofar as you share Christ's sufferings." In other words, your sufferings are not merely your own. They are also Christ's. This is cause for rejoicing because it means you are united to Christ.

Joseph Tson, a Romanian pastor who stood up to Ceausescu's repressions of Christianity, wrote,

> *This union with Christ is the most beautiful subject in the Christian life. It means that I am not a*

lone fighter here: I am an extension of Jesus Christ. When I was beaten in Romania, he suffered in my body. It is not my suffering: I only had the honor to share his sufferings (undated paper: "A Theology of Martyrdom").

Keep on rejoicing, because your sufferings as a Christian are not merely yours but Christ's and they give evidence of your union with him.

3. A Means to Attaining Greater Joy in Glory

Keep on rejoicing because this joy will strengthen your assurance that when Christ comes in glory, you will rejoice forever with him.

Verse 13b: "But rejoice insofar as you share Christ's sufferings, that you may also rejoice and be glad when his glory is revealed." Notice: keep on rejoicing now, so that you may rejoice then. Our joy now through suffering is the means of attaining our joy then, a thousand-fold in glory.

First there is suffering, then there is glory. 1 Peter 1:11, "The Spirit predicted the sufferings of Christ and the glory to follow" (cf. 5:1). Paul said, "If we suffer with him we will be glorified with him." First the suffering, and then the glory—both for Jesus and for those who are united to him.

If we become embittered at life and the pain it deals us, we are not preparing to rejoice at the revelation of Christ's glory. Keep on rejoicing now in suffering in order that you might rejoice with exultation at the revelation of his glory.

4. The Spirit of Glory and of God Rest on You

Keep on rejoicing in suffering because then the Spirit of glory and of God rest upon you.

Verse 14: "If you are insulted for the name of Christ, you are blessed, because the Spirit of glory and of God rests upon you."

This means that in the hour of greatest trial there is a great consolation. In great suffering on earth there is great support from heaven. You may think now that you will not be able to bear it. But if you are Christ's, you will be able to bear it, because he will come to you and rest upon you. As Rutherford said, the Great King keeps his finest wine in the cellar of affliction. He does not bring it out to serve with chips on sunny afternoons. He keeps it for extremities.

If you say, "What is this?"—the Spirit of glory and of God resting on me in suffering—the answer is simply this: you will find out when you need it. The Spirit will reveal enough of glory and enough of God to satisfy your soul, and carry you through.

Seek to be holy; seek to bring truth; seek to bear witness; and do not turn aside from risk. And sooner or later you will experience the Spirit of glory and of God resting upon you in suffering.

5. Rejoicing in Suffering Glorifies God

Keep on rejoicing in suffering because this glorifies God.

Verse 16: "If anyone suffers as a Christian, let him not be ashamed, but let him glorify God in that name."

Glorifying God means showing by your actions and attitudes that God is glorious to you—that he is valuable, precious, desirable, satisfying. And the greatest way to show that someone satisfies your heart is to keep on rejoicing in them when all other supports for your satisfaction are falling away. When you keep rejoicing in God in the midst of suffering, it shows that God, and not other things, is the great source of your joy.

Remember Paul Brand, the missionary surgeon to India. He tells the story of his mother who was a missionary in India and who did something that symbolizes a life devoted through suffering to the glory of God and not self. Dr. Brand writes,

> *For Mother, pain was a frequent companion, as was sacrifice. I say it kindly and in love, but in old age, Mother had little of physical beauty left in her. The rugged conditions, combined with the crippling falls and her battles with typhoid, dysentery, and malaria, had made her a thin, hunched-over old woman. Years of exposure to wind and sun had toughened her facial skin into leather and furrowed it with wrinkles as deep and extensive as any I have seen on a human face... Mother knew that as well as anyone—for the last 20 years of her life she refused to keep a mirror in her house* (Christianity Today, *Jan. 10, 1994, 23).*

Twenty years of ministry without a mirror. Do you get it? She was the mirror. God was the light and the glory.

6. God's Faithfulness to Care for Your Soul

Finally, keep on rejoicing because your Creator is faithful to care for your soul.

Verse 19: "Therefore let those who suffer according to God's will entrust their souls to a faithful Creator while doing good."

The degrees of suffering and the forms of affliction will differ for every one of us. But one thing we will all have in common till Jesus comes: we will all die. We will come to that awesome moment of reckoning. If you have time, you will see your whole life played before you as you ponder if it has been well-spent. You will tremble at the unspeakable reality that in just moments you will face God. And the destiny of your soul will be irrevocable.

Will you rejoice in that hour? You will if you entrust your soul to a faithful Creator. He created your soul for his glory. He is faithful to that glory and to all who love it and live for it. Now is the time to show where your treasure is—in heaven or on earth. Now is the time to shine with the glory of God. Trust him. And keep on rejoicing.

NOTES

1 Jonathan Edwards, "God Glorified in the Work of Redemption, by the Greatness of Man's Dependence upon Him, in the Whole of It (1731)" [sermon on 1 Corinthians 1:29-31] in: Wilson H. Kimnach, Kenneth P. Minkema, and Douglas A. Sweeney, ed., *The Sermons of Jonathan Edwards: A Reader* (New Haven: Yale University Press, 1999), 74–75.

2 Katherine Hankey (1834–1911), "Tell Me the Old, Old Story."

3 These details are based on an article from Tom Steller, February 28, 1995.

4 Peter Morden, Offering Christ to the World (Waynesboro, Georgia: Paternoster, 2003), 167.

desiringGod

The mission of Desiring God is that people everywhere would understand and embrace the truth that God is most glorified in us when we are most satisfied in him. Our primary strategy for accomplishing this mission is through a maximally useful website that houses over thirty years of John Piper's preaching and teaching, including translations into more than 40 languages. This is all available free of charge, thanks to our generous ministry partners. If you would like to further explore the vision of Desiring God, we encourage you to visit www.desiringGod.org.

Desiring God

Post Office Box 2901, Minneapolis, Minnesota 55402

888.346.4700 mail@desiringGod.org

7612281R00112

Printed in Great Britain
by Amazon.co.uk, Ltd.,
Marston Gate.

learning gravity

poetry

helen oswald

tall-lighthouse

Acknowledgements are due to the editors of the following publications where some of these poems first appeared: *Poetry Review, Magma, Poetry London, The Rialto, Stand, P.N. Review, London Magazine, Reactions 1* and *2*.

I would also like to thank the many people who have provided invaluable support and advice over the years: Maura Dooley, Simon Jenner, Roddy Lumsden, John McCullough, Esther Morgan, Andrew Motion and John Stammers.

Vacation, The Dark Skies Society and *Brighton Pavilion* were commended respectively in the 1999, 2000 & 2009 National Poetry Competition.

Morning After was a runner up in the Bridport Prize 2009.

Inventing Zero was a winner and *Lost Language* was commended in the Arvon International Poetry Competition 2004.

Learning Gravity was a winner of the Blue Nose Poets-of-the-Year Competition 1999.

cover image: hicky2 – designyourway.net

cover photo: Emily Bolam

published 2010
ISBN 978 1 904551 77 5
www.tall-lighthouse.co.uk

contents

In memory of my brother

(Paul Oswald 1958 – 1992)

In the Beginning

My mother used to leave me
out under a lemon tree, wriggling
bug-like on my back, dandled
in the black carapace of my pram.
I must have stared up and seen
those bright yellow shapes suspended,
looked and looked and thought nothing,
acquainting myself with the facts,
the pure essence of lemonhood,
before the word molded
itself from formless sounds.
Now I have the label 'lemon'
pinned all over that tree.
It is the one thing
that separates those lemons and me.

Ordering Genes

We are what our grandparents ate.
Their choices from the cold store ordered my genes
so that a grapefruit dissected with the proper tool
and eaten by my grandma on the eve of war
accounts for this bitterness I sometimes feel.

And maybe that extra cow's-lick of butter
churned from grandpa's Irish herd,
scooped up on his initialled silver blade
passed down to my own cutlery drawer,
has marked me too; my slick, emollient tongue.

I have no children of my own
but today I select with care: mussels in their shells,
unscrubbed; hake, the deep sea gleam
still polished in its eye; tomatoes not yet ripe,
their stubborn grip on the vine.

The Passion

That year it made a change from cowboys and indians,
my brother's hyena yelp as he scalped me again.
Comanche. We knew about the thrill of blood.

Out in the greenhouse, we sawed wooden stakes
recast from former roles piercing the hearts
of vampires, to nail three crosses.

I tore old bed sheets into strips of loincloth,
anointed the feet of a bear with Pears shampoo
and left it overnight in a geranium Gethsemane.

Our reluctant parents watched
at an upstairs window, mortified and yet
unable to wash their hands of it.

Beneath the holly tree that had supplied
a crown of thorns, two gollies, thieves,
awaited Christ, and me and my brother

stretched to an unruly crowd, yelling:
"Crucify him! Crucify him!"
Two small gods making it all happen.

Sunday School Outing

The boy from the new estate
drifted out asleep,
his two-tone lilo
sipped at the horizon.

He had failed to keep
our Union Jack umbrella
in his sights. We lined up
to bellow his unfamiliar name.

My brother swam far out
after someone else's child.
My mother begged the ocean
for two specks re-emerging.

We drove straight home.
No dodgems, no doughnuts,
no sugar on our hands.

Air Raid, Coventry 1940

My mother implores the bombs
even now to hush,
go back to sleep.

Fifty years on, she has been to see
the new cathedral burst
from a burnt seed.

Memories explode as she describes
banshee sirens, the low drone of planes,
swastikas spidering their bellies.

She was a girl that night the sky turned red.
I have never been so terrified, she says.
Well, I have. But I hadn't then.

The house shook, as her voice shakes now.
They stood in the hall and listened
to thuds, *like someone falling*.

Her mother was afraid to leave.
All night they watched their world quake.
Portraits jitterbugged against the walls.

She tells me all this, but she does not tell me
what terrified her since. Silence
detonates in the space between us.

Full Tilt

We spent our lives falling off bikes.
Jab's Hill was breakneck steep, your brakes jammed
racing to that fete; you sliced across a major road
like scissors through ribbon.

Remember the night you switched off your lights
flying back from music school, using moonbeams instead?
You forgot about clouds. We found the fiddle in the ditch
days later, cushioned in its coffin.

Or the time we cycled two abreast? No hands.
The handlebars locked horns and joined us at the hip
until we came apart, you and I,
like a book falling open.

One Day on the Moon

My father said, *Look!*
That man is walking on the moon.
It was barely one year
since I first felt the earth
tilt up to teach me a lesson.

This man then, bouncing,
was not doing it right,
walking was not like that.
You lifted the weight of your life
and balanced it on one leg.

My father said, *One day*
on the moon lasts
fourteen on earth.
A day to me was half a lifetime,
a fortnight, infinity.

I turned away from the moon
and the man floating
in his white romper suit
and buried my face
in the hinge of my father's knee.

He is dead now.
I am middle-aged.
I understand all things
fall with equal speed in a vacuum.

The Dark Skies Society

What they wanted was less light,
less light and the chance to look up
to see tonight's old stars shining
and dying. Dark skies and fewer
street lamps leaking Lucozade
into a space once reserved
for heaven where they might glimpse
Venus opening her door a crack
or, leaning out of an upstairs window,
overhear God making plans in verse,
honing the moon into half-rhyme.

They believed – and said they had proved it –
that light pollution could cause cancer,
near-sightedness, insomnia and for some
drug addiction. They understood the heart
needs a dark place to thump undetected,
to go underground like a badger, burrowing
its own blind streets, to back out unseen
into fields where the beet sweetens.

Inventing Zero

It's not my fault.
Camels in. Camels out.
And then Zudin,
he comes with empty hands
this man who snubs the gods.

If it was up to me
I'd ignore it, but the priests
they check the columns,
and I have spent my life
learning how to count.

I have to put something
but he brings nothing,
not a sheep, nor even a loaf.
How do I record
the camel that is not there?

In the gap that is Zudin's
refusal to pay homage
I put a sign – two diagonals –
in the hope it fails
to catch their eyes.

Tonight, I sit by the Tigris
thinking of the mark
I have made –
the name of the void.
Is this what a man can do?

Down by the reeds I see Zudin
laughing and throwing stones
from the bank, oblivious
to the reckoning, the shape
I have given nothing.

Silk Purse

These are the last coins you carried in your pocket.
You travelled light.

Never one to stay in any place for long in life
or put down roots.

And yet you recognised the urge to roll out
golf courses, like carpets,

or the need to enter a house to escape
the wide-eyed sky.

But you refused to stitch the old sow's ear.
You wanted out.

The night you fell
all the king's horses were locked in their stables.

These monarchs' heads return to me intact –
hard currency.

All Saints, South Cadbury

Stiff faces spill from cars into silence,
herd up the churchyard, shy away like sheep.
It's hard to believe the same crowd danced
all through a London night and fell asleep
under the sky's marquee at Andrew's wedding
last July. We blew across the park – bright,
crumpled litter – and drove home laughing.

Now we are all wide awake but chalk white,
standing beside the hole we want to shun.
Suddenly you're there in my dry mind's eye,
raising your wine glass – a wry oration,
wishing the newly-weds good luck, goodbye.
The mute grave catches my breath, mouth open
it welcomes your tongue. Every word spoken.

Letter from Above Ground

In the distance, the Downs turn green.
Trees feather their nests,
stretch a trapeze of skinny births.
Some will fall without a safety net.

Seagulls show their white crowns to the sky,
dapple the roofs with shit.
There is a gravity that pulls all things
to the earth and under it.

And yet the planet hurtles on.
Sunday. The kettle cools its breath.
I wash my hair, dead already,
but note a slippery virulence.

Trains sashay across the viaduct
batting their eyes at the sun.
The arches long to cool their thighs
in the sea beyond. Their day may come.

On tennis courts, balls rock back and forth
swung in a cat's cradle of white lines.
You used to play but never kept score.
Fifteen, thirty love. No more.

Chilled

One wine voucher, still valid,
pulled from your things
like a body, still breathing,
from a shelled building.

I choose a young, white Burgundy
that has not had time to mature
and, for a moment, I'm unsure
before I ease the cork and pour.

Test for Porcelain

The guy on *eBay* claimed his restored Ming
was stronger; that trauma
glued back together bonds longer.

He stipulated tools and colours: clamps
to hold things under pressure;
burnt umber, rose madder, cobalt aurora.

In the West, the test for porcelain
is translucence, but in China
they listen for the ring it makes

when tapped – a perfect pitch.
Would the mended one, when struck,
not sound its broken heritage?

The Brink

The dog's detective nose
sticks into ditches,
picks up clues, forensic.

Cows chew cud, rough tongues
talk to themselves about milk,
days melt in their mouths.

A flutter of birds starts
to chat about flight,
strung out at the brink.

Learning Gravity

i.

Now you are bones.
The whole puppet show
has clattered from your hands.
Death stops all machinery.

You are a Christmas toy
in a box, without a battery.
I must wait for the shops to open,
I must wait an eternity.

Now I am almost your age,
in one year you will be younger.
After all our games, all our races,
I am the winner; I am the loser.

ii.

Here is the very chair, outliving you
as all the props outlive us all, a warning
on the balcony
to the leaning trees.

You sit patiently with me, waiting
to be given back your shape
in some strange way,
don't you think?

That summer we sunbathed in the garden
and came inside peeling. Beneath the skin
the new pink infant
born from the day's burning.

iii.

We are driving down
to the Deep South.

A constant felling of pines
and raising up of timber.

As we approach,
giant yellow M's leapfrog forest,

the sun's eye catches
tin-can cars. Highways

tie the city in knots.
It shimmers, celestial mirage,

narcissistic towers of mirrored glass
admire reflections.

Sweet dreams and sour cream,
dollar, dolour, duller.

All you can eat.

iv.

You declined it all and instead
selected an apple for your last meal.
You bit to the core and balanced
what was left, spiked with pips
on the ledge, taking the rootless flesh
into the ground for planting.

But I still live in this city where the sun
gold-plates the west side of Canary Wharf,
flashing its light to no rocks, no sea.
The Cutty Sark remains cemented in dry dock,
the crystal heart of Docklands beats
and I piece you back together in my mind.

v.

I guess this is loss, you said,
staring through the glass-bottomed boat
at the drowned town: dammed, filled up.
Hefts of water press into spaces
opened up for air; free passage
for word, look, touch, footfall.

A spire fingers the hull. We avoid puncture
and sail on. Slates are washed black
by perpetual downpour; a hearth gargles
as we pass, a chimney swallows,
water settles deeper. *No fish*, you say.
Yes, and no dove either.

vi.

Your clothes hang, become the person
you stopped being.

Your camera misses the breathtaking scene
that requires no living.

Your books talk to themselves, every page
recalls your face.

Your music is unplayed, dumb, inaudible
even to dogs.

vii.

I am reading your horoscope.
The Sun and Mars remain in your sign,
you are flooded with solar power.
The sky is junked with satellites
but I believe it.

The world is lit by two full moons this month.
Keep your head down. Do not become entangled
in half-truths. A beautiful aspect
between Venus and Saturn
looks promising now.

You must remember: happiness
comes only when you look
the other way; love
when you least need it.
This day is a rare one for you.

viii.

The last leaf drops,
breaks its back coming down,
lands, dead as a stunt man.

Later, snow will settle
and soles will print
the skeletons of fish.

But afternoon keeps still,
holds every living thing
nailed to the second-hand planet.

Wrecked, Solitary, Here

'I felt a Funeral, in my Brain…' Emily Dickinson

Days when the spinning ball
whirls in my head, fast and blurred
like those windmills held as a child,

I long for the all-knowing
IT guy – someone to say,
hit Control-Alt-Delete.

And I think of Dickinson
and her meticulous basket
let down to the world.

I google her, thirsty
for washed-up messages
from a bottled heart;

or a nursery rhyme mystic –
Blake mourning innocence,
those voices on the green...

Both of them still calling
clear across the low-tech centuries
their god-blown incantations.

The Melt

Initially, there was euphoria at winter's first coat;
cold, bright stitches sewing everything up.

But it was the fresh revelation as the melt began
that made the familiar appear far worse than before.

The bared spines of roof ridges, cars' exoskeletons
anaesthetised in ice, reawakening. Everywhere
white robes

slipping open. A loss of privacy, unmissed in the night,
left a sense of shame. In city gardens it seemed

another Eden was defiled. Emerging grass delivered
a green shock beneath decrepit trees. Driving to work

behind the gritter, we saw a short blessing withdrawn
as the street's rough elephant skin resurfaced.

Love Affair with Limes

You had the guts to drink them
diluted only with white rum –
the barman selecting a tough glass,
stamping a pestle hard to free
a green fruit's acid tang.

Crushed ice pressed tight against
naked, citrus skin. Salt crystals glinted
around the rim. I watched your head tilt
to swallow a brew close to nitro-glycerine.
Inside my chest, a slow explosion.

Second Language

Acting hostess, I am keeping you at bay
with, *How long have you been here?* And,
What have you seen so far?

You, you say. *I have seen you*.

I laugh, startled. You smile,
pleased to cause shock in another tongue
as your careful fingers seem to tie a knot.

Through the Curtain

I imagine you flying east,
a contraband of empty jars
hidden among T-shirts, jeans, bras;
eggs incubating in the interior
beneath rows of reclining seats.

This delicate feast you choose
to carry home. The jars, glass coffins
for your mother's plums, walnuts, gherkins;
the eggs to last her till spring
because there's nothing once winter sets in.

You were ashamed and proud
to own your illicit cargo. I prayed
your frail, white bird safely through the clouds
to lay its eggs. This soft trade
breaks embargoes, brokers love's peace.

Night Flight

At the airport, your lips
pull, duty free, on a fag. Resolve slips.

Tonight touch shocks, returns
everything lost. Love burns.

In sleep, you cross into bilingual dreams,
you have more homes than one it seems.

You show up quarterly on the phone bill,
my voice has entered unseen cities at will.

You and I exist in flight,
between arrival, departure, delight.

Vacation

Everything was spread too thin except the air
which wobbled, full of rain about to slop
on spongy fields yielding nothing but earth,
translated into turf at one remove.

Our car spun out a shiny web of roads.
I think we hoped to trap a town
where we might catch ourselves
reflected dimly in shop windows.

Instead, that awful mountain, Errigal,
jutting like a buried monster's rotted knee,
made us ants, dragging crumbs
of dead religions twice our weight.

It held us in its sights across flat miles of bog,
breaking weak talk of weddings and new jobs,
leaving its mark in you, a prune-black bruise
you lost all hope of healing.

Home Entertainment

No, let's stay home, let me be your circus.
From our ceiling I'll string a trapeze, dangle
upside down in lycra by my toes, conjure
two tigers to crouch by your feet – see their teeth
bare, danger shine in an eye. I will wear
a dinner jacket to tame them, walk on my hands
through mid air, cartwheel up walls, juggle
six lit candles. You will applaud of course.

Before you can get bored, I will fold
pages of the Sunday paper into falcons,
perch them on picture rails. That carpet
is wasted on the floor, I'll get it airborne.
Climb up! Let's visit the kitchen, shrink
in a hot wash, go sailing in the sink.
The freezer is ripe for arctic exploration:
we'll scale the Birds Eye peaks, race to the Pole.

Through with showbiz we will retire,
punch flat our black top hats, shake off
our tails and spill the guts of pillows to make
a nest of curled, white feathers for our bed.
We'll hang curtains at our heads and feet,
rig a four-poster fit for Henry VIII
and half a dozen wives. Come,
let's have the time of our lives.

Morning After

Sunday slicks in.
Unwoken by light
you lie in dreams.
Your bags are packed.

Romance is a parrot –
I love you, I love you.
It parodies what cannot be put
into words, or cages.

Last night more was said
by the soft snow of parmesan,
a bright sprig of parsley
to freshen the breath.

Now we rock along the tracks.
The carriage draws
a thick line through this town.
Conversation sticks.

In Battersea, jailed dogs
yap at the quiet power station,
idling on its back,
legs to heaven.

At Victoria, your train door
bangs shut. The smack of sound
hits us and you slam on your smile
like a brake.

Not Wanting to Write about Truffles

Inside my head, the image hunkers down: terriers
sniff out musty chunks nestled at the roots
stinking of dry rot. These dogs have a nose
for what hides deep in the earth's architecture.

Once loosed, the truffles loom up like space junk
behind the credits of a sci-fi movie – inscrutable
in their particular mix of matter and air,
survivors of an ugly, knock-about game.

In this odd, acquired taste there is something rare
but not quite right. They are tumours that once cut out
offer only a short reprieve; the Reaper's stolen goods.

Their value is not in scarcity but in that saving,
exhuming delicacies from dead ground.
Try as I may, I still go down there with the hope of it.

Against the Pane

This light diviner frisks December glass,
shivers with desire for summer nights.

Cold now, wings half shut,
it dies for the hot stroke of July.

If I touch it, a silvery print
might make me think of angels' wings.

No. I turn my back and press hard
into the dark months ahead.

New Year, IKEA

After we'd snuffed the wick of talk,
we joined a caravan of hatchbacks
crawling on Purley Way to reach
the mouth of a blind megastore.

Inside, we aped a mausoleum crowd
ogling dead display models – couches
where life was laid out before us,
virgin bath tubs yawning beside loos

where queasy Bacchus never kneels.
None of this appealed. Further in,
unploughed beds stretched out
cold, white fields and pillows drifted,

unimpressed by dreaming heads
or jealous bears. We moved on
to a room where tools evolved
for kitchen autopsies glittered.

Steering for home, a grapefruit sun
squeezed pink juice on the horizon
but we could find no words
beyond 'lovely'.

Sinking into the torn familiar
TV sofa, we watched *The Pyramids*.
Old kings hoarding treasure
to do it all again later, better.

A Raven's Bones

The house is saturated, the smell of must
pervades each room. We squelch outside

picking our way between rusting barbeques.
I cannot help thinking of the English

tramping around the tropics in rotting brogues,
flushing their veins with gin

and quinine to put mosquitoes off their blood.
This sort of summer slouches in with a grudge,

the sun floats like a bad egg, refusing to shine,
a warning of change to come.

Once, at a party, a guy pulled from his pocket
a tiny bag rolled like stowed hash

to flaunt a scrap of wood he swore
his mate found in a dig for Noah's Ark.

I don't know if it's true or not,
it's the fact that they are out there

clawing through the mud of Ararat
for splinters of cypress, a raven's bones.

It cheers me as I watch a window's beauty
blurred by a cawl of rain.

The Meet

A clot of pink coats turned
the market square to blood.
I felt compelled to witness again
the ancient brute tableau,

to view the twitchy horses, arses
polished to a conker's gleam;
to study flushed Dickensian faces,
wild eyes all round, ready

to cheer or heckle the master,
up in his stirrups for a speech
against the ban or for the Queen
before they gallop off. Unleashed,

gangly hounds slather saliva,
nostrils all out for fear's musky scent,
ears cocked for the horn's yelp –
a creature already trapped.

Its first shriek whips
the tangle of bone and sinew
frenzied across iced fields.
Four-by-fours growl in the lane.

Under a damp shirt, my heart
bolts. Deep in its cells it knows
there is always this pursuit.
Someone blooded, run to ground.

Stamp

Strange how those old dictators
banished their own heads
from the currency of mail,
exhibiting instead a taste for butterflies,
hibiscus and highly-coloured birds.

They never licked or stuck
but left that to their people.
I think of all those mouths glued shut
sending out perforated ambassadors
to decorate the globe.

Remembrance Monday

Back on leave with the kids, he must bite his lip
when ice cream tastes of innocence, whipped.

Not notice the empty cone, hollow as a bone,
the marrow sucked out far from home.

Forget that dodgems sparking and colliding
ignite memories of a city imploding;

that this beach reeks of hot flesh and petrol,
the sour sweat of a soldier's next patrol.

Keeping an Eye

I am the sort they ask to keep an eye
when popping to the loo on trains.
I nod and smile then slide
across the aisle; throw on
her cashmere coat, turn up
the fake fur collar, grab her
Louis Vuitton calf-skin bag –
its tiny bronze padlock,
its vulnerable seams.
I leave my old skin
neatly folded in her seat,
hop off at the next stop,
wish her luck.

Allotments

i.

This plot had been abandoned. Its meagre spoils
deterred even the toughest allotment stock.
In front, waves lapped the flats at Whitehawk,
their tangled cables charged through our topsoil.
We unearthed White Lightning cans, rusty perks
of neglect. Behind, on the racecourse, pounding
hooves beneath blurred jockeys made ground
quake under our feet and drove us back to work.

Each sod was like a mattress, full of dust,
horsehair – and hogweed. It has rights here,
grip, takes over when we give up the nurture
of short-lived, pretty stuff; needs no compost.
It perseveres where our blistered hands
are always slowly slipping off this land.

ii.

Today's warm breeze, a glider, imports spring.
Bees fly in, their droning engines nuzzle the willow's
blonde powdered wig. The honey locust slaps its brow
unravelling the anagram on the tip of its tongues
all winter: l-e-a-v-e-s. Round by the dustbins
forsythia's gone over the top defining 'yellow',
sucking up to the sun. Cherry blossom makes a bow
then dissolves like candy floss. In the distance, the wind
tickles my washing, doubling up a row of me, curled
as if I'd finally got the joke. The whole performance
conjures that old comedian throwing the same punch
year after year, *Jus' like that,* and we crack up fondly;
or that overplayed love song that means the world
to you and me. Killing us, but killing us softly.

iii.

All day long we'd slogged in hot sun, dreaming
of chilled beers to come, never working
for its own reward but planting for yield,
sweating to replace hot fluids with cold
fizzing gold. A ditched seagull chick was not
what we had toiled for, but there he sat,
his squawk half formed, his fluff not quite
yet feathers. His first flight crashed to patio.

Our rescue bid produced a panicked
half-flight, half-hop to next door. We sank a jar
but couldn't relax as the jasmine shone its stars
and we watched for cats. But in the night, the chick
decoded the hieroglyphics of his sky-built DNA,
mastered a frail technology and flapped away.

Arcadia

You sleep beside me.
The car is set on autocruise.
I drive and drive until it seems
this is an arcade game –
the unravelling road,
the barely controlled car.

Sleep is a danger
so I start to dream of what lies
behind those endless Georgia pines:
I catch a glimpse of fields –
a bromide residue remains,
I think I see the scrag of cotton heads.

My mind begins to populate
the land with black slave labour.
The thought feels kitschy, fake,
like those porcelain models
of 'colored folk' at prayer
we saw for sale in Atlanta.

I summon Native Americans
stalking between tall trunks –
underfoot, a snapped twig
lethal as a gunshot.
But the drama won't play out,
my head sprouts a Mohican cliché.

Another car passes,
its occupants mute, staring ahead,
and I recall the flight over here.
Above the clouds, that nowhere place
just like the heaven people dreamed of
before they got off the ground.

Return Ticket

It still bothers me, though days have passed since
that ordinary morning's shapeshift – the instant
we were sucked into the tunnel, an answering
gasp of breath from a clutch of lungs.

Torn from the bruised spring, edged
with cracked crocus buds leaking yolk,
we pierced earth's skin and made our entry
into darkness; an invasive surgery.

The temperature dropped, an odour of wet rock,
must in our throats; practice for a breathless future.
Then, eyes wide as newborns', we burst back out
into a bluebell wood jangling nature's bling.

At Gatwick, I blessed the Trojan birds swooping
down to tarmac, cloud still tangled in their feet.
Trackside, up in an oak, even a captive Asda bag
opened its mouth and drew a deep slug of air.

To Kyoto

Encased in our bullet, we assumed
the weightlessness of astronauts
defying laws. Brittle trees jumped,
towns streaked across the plains.

Further down the line, they had got out.
Cows. Heads hard as rock, soft bodies
swaying in a milky motion towards
the liquid promise of grass.

Our carriage stopped further back.
We walked down the track,
eyes locked high in the maples.
What reached us was the smell of blood.

Kite

Would it have helped if I had told you
the way to fly a kite is not straight up?
Rein in the wind with cautious tugs,
chance a coy ripple, court rebuff.
Above all, suspend disbelief.

Should I have said, look at it like this –
birds flatter the wind with wings
then fly in fast, a boxer in the ring,
deal a sly uppercut, head tucked flush
to the shoulder; their power featherweight.

Sometimes the wind drops down low,
scuffles through grass like a spaniel,
nose clamped hard to the scent.
That was when we lost you,
when you entertained descent.

The Element of Air

Lisbon, 1709

I recall the thin smattering
of applause, the court tittering
behind fans at this dreamer,
Bartolomeu de Gusmão, trying
to get to heaven in a hot paper bag.

His absurd contraption hovered
above his majesty's head.
We kept a watchful eye
for a yawn or frown, indicating
dinner or displeasure.

But Gusmão did not care.
He contemplated a flaming bird
scorching the air, the climax
of decades singeing his fingers
to rise above we 'lead-boot critics'.

Rumours spread: his *Short Manifesto*
for those unaware it is possible to sail
through the element of air
might rile the Inquisition. Deep down
we suspected this ambition.

He fled to Toledo and died of a fever.
So much for 'combustion'.
A lesson for our children –
keep your feet on *terra firma*
only angels sail in air.

Brighton Pavilion

In the end, we never made it to the Pavilion
but preferred instead to imagine
the gauche chinoiserie of Regency folly,
a camp flourish of minarets standing out
against the bitter English rain.

We closed our eyes and conjured faux Indian
domes knocked out from a nation's first
concrete casts – brown and smooth
and looking, for all they're worth,
like cardboard.

We paused to consider the pooh-poohing
of hoi polloi; their descendants
even now slinging mud at anyone
daring to aspire – the crowd
who would throw Tesco up for Kubla Khan.

We meant to come in praise of whatever it is
that insists against the odds upon gilding
a dolphin on a lampstand, that craves
primrose rooms and chandeliers shaped
like fuchsia blooms hung upside down.

But most of all, we liked to picture
a garden inspired by a glutton whose devotion
transported peonies, erected hollyhocks.
We see ourselves drowsing among his poppies,
seduced by the scent of blousy stocks.

Patience

You know the name
of every bone in my anatomy
and point out, gently,
my *supraclavicular fossa*.

You lower your head expertly
onto the shipwreck of my ribs,
explain that though my heartbeat
is irregular, there is no danger.

Tender exploration tells you
by what tool and what technique
the midwife cut me from my mother
that torpid morning in Tunisia.

I listen patiently, dying to defy
your dictionary. At last,
when we are wordless, I touch
the simple language of your body.

Rough Work

The damp, sweet, Southern summer
thickens like syrup, turns chapters
of our holiday novels into pancakes.

High in the pines, a shrill persistence
keens some forest loss unknown to us.
We are visitors here.

Unseen in the half-light, a blade
tears at the air, slices silence,
cuts through our time

so that soon we will find
our days piled up like logs.
Rough work done for the winter.

Leaving the City

Step up out of Brighton to the Downs,
ignore the race horses' jittery dashes,
let traffic subside and skylarks unspool,
watch silvery jets slide overhead.

Fling yourself down among vetch's bonnets,
campanula's mutton-chop sleeves, the studs
of blown ragwort. This fitness is not designed
to flex the calves, it picks the heart's locks.

Coming back down through seasick wheat,
Seven Sisters flash lace skirts, Lewes emerges
shaken from a mirage. It's no mean feat now
to cross the highway's queasy footbridge.

The Honey Locust

It's rarely as lovely as you think. Lunch outside
under the honey locust tree, its arms waving
in what you suppose is some kind of blessing
encouraging a gazing up into the blue, until

whatever the hell the builders are doing
next door erupts. A grinding persists for months
inside and out. Their renovations jar
hairline cracks all through this summer's peace.

It's always like that. Trying to conjure
moments of rapture snatches them away. Instead
it was those unexpected seconds in the lounge
gripping the pile tight beneath bare toes

that brought the frisson, the gathering of what
hovers in the peripheral vision or slides, mercurial
in that vapour above the water in my glass, offering
just a shimmer, diffusing the edge of thought.

And wording it is a dubious business. The hope
that the tweezering in of the tiniest parts
through this bottle's narrow neck is equal
to the real craft out there, steering a muddy Channel,

endeavouring to balance itself at the precise point
between here, the horizon, the stone-strewn depth
and its own inky shadow
doodling the back of the moon's retina.

The Fishermen of Malaga

These *Malagueños* rob their sea and lay it out
grievous, bodily, drowned in oil, disguised
in breaded coats or raw. *Bacalao frito,*
muslitos de cangrejo, torito camarones...

All summoned by a shout, carried head high,
plates dealt out like aces onto upturned barrels;
and *fino*, dry as the sand scouring the English
on the beach, slopped with a generous hand.

It takes time to learn to hit the tapas tide
when dealers open up and the town shifts
obliquely towards a narrow door. We arrived
too early in empty bars, awkward and alone

until, like crabs on a shore, they were everywhere
roused by light crashing onto empty streets,
ready to extricate lives from shells,
to taste the day's catch, sweet and cruel.

Lost Language

Perhaps they lived their lives out passing notes,
pointing at the salt and pepper – *ecloog* and *ecclute* –
unspoken words struggling for air, lolling on the tongue
until death closed its lips on the lexicon, a withered fruit.

It had to be a row that killed it. The last utterance
of what I shall call *Umbetka* in my language, going to its grave
in a state of rage, escorted by an exclamation mark – §.
The last *Umbetkazi* struck dumb by the given offence.

It hangs somewhere, that final phrase; what, I will never know.
I never spoke *Umbetka* nor could describe its proper name,
only the silence that followed and the thought of their funerals
conducted volubly by a neighbouring tribe.

And, now their lips are mulched back to the bone, their books
back to the logs they came from, would their god
still understand their prayer if from the wastes of limbo
they called out to her – *Oustare§* – in a loud voice?

New Pitch

Hungry for new ground, heartsick for the old,
the Millwall fans crash in fresh from The Den,
tight with disallowed tears, ripped up turf, goals
fit to burst: the last match lost. Englishmen.
Ill-advised bar staff deny them and duck.
They pick up stools and fling them at a glare
of mirrors, wreck The Mayflower pub. *Fuck
you, bastards!* Fast arms flash, reflections tear,
the air cracks and rings, rains glass – shards sparkle
like smash-and-grab diamonds. Pints jostle, spill,
hit the deck and break into wet petals.
Time slows right down and stops. We watch them, still,
as silence falls, dumb with fascination,
while sirens hail their brilliant destruction.

Deep Fielder

I saw you at dawn walking between rooms
lit by flashes ripped from an electric storm.
Wet air fused blue around your face
raised to greet or say goodbye.

I did not know you, but your eyes
caught mine as light is caught
and held in a glass vase, or a ball
smacks into the palm of a deep fielder.

Daylight Saving

The sun is leaving light,
like oil, on the water.

Couples kiss in silhouette
as clouds burn rubber and skid to a halt.

Waves mutter and sigh, a restless crowd
liable to riot, stampede across shingle.

A goalie, diving between posts, becomes luminous,
almost makes a save.

Leaving the Island

The sick child's face shines in my head like the moon.
I search for a cure by the shore
as tides tease out hope and drag it back under.
All day, the useless petulant sea has thrown itself at land
like a distraught wife, clutching a hem of sand.
I turn with empty hands and slog back through thick mud.

The supple trees bend to our will and are felled.
We split the pulpy white trunks by the water's edge,
run a cut up their bellies and gut them like cod. Ships!
The word is lodged in the inner ear, in shells.
I stand with my back to the sodden land.
I smell spice; cures in the salt wind.

We light fires on the sand to celebrate –
they burn so hard and hot the shore has turned to glass.
Our bleeding hands smear the rough stern. We push
as if to turn the world, have rigged the garb off our backs.
My eel child slithers from my grip and slips between
briny legs. Our sails are thumped by a gust and winded.

~

I was chosen to go. They said: *You are a stargazer,*
you will steer a steady course through night waters.
I have left the pale child slung beneath another breast.
All milk tastes the same to me. I lean out and admire
jewels on the ocean's black chest.

The days are bad. I dream of the greens of oak,
yew and elder, of flame and frost. I miss my flinty land.
Sometimes I think I see this flat, grey pan of sea
narrow to an estuary, a silvery river
tinged with iron and the faint taste of blood.

Oranges and lemons. I put out my tongue and squeeze.
The droplets run in gullies down my throat,
the way our ship slipped with relief into each new land
stretched out, warm as a lover in bed.

How can I describe the pock of orange skin,
a lemon's nipple, the oyster wince of impact on my tongue?
And coconut, a hairy breast of milk.

I dress in the warm breeze of a summer evening
which is called silk. Colours are wrung from the rainbow
to dye my clothes. Laden like thieves
we will carry these miracles home and be welcomed
like gods.